FAVOUR
Dimension

IFEOMA
R. FIIRITER

The
FAVOUR
*D*imension

IFEOMA
R. FIIRITER

THE FAVOUR DIMENSION

ISBN 978-1-907143-25-0

Published by Favour Land Publications
April 2018
5 Keswick Close, Ardwick,
Manchester
M13 0DD
United Kingdom

Table of Contents

ACKNOWLEDGEMENT

I praise God for giving me the grace to receive from Him the revelations about divine favour contained in this book, **The Favour Dimension,** with the ability to also write and publish it.

I thank God for giving me the privilege to co-labour with Him to minister His anointing of favour upon the lives of many people in dire straits, some of whose testimonies of breakthrough I share in this book.

I thank God for all the spiritual, physical, financial and material resources He provided to help us successfully publish this life-changing book.

I also thank God for Rev. Daniel Fiiriter, my husband, whose love and dedicated support helped in the editing and publication of this great work. I pray that God will continually increase you in wisdom and stature and in favour with God and men. May He also perfect all that concerns you.

INTRODUCTION!

Do you really understand what divine favour is, and how powerful it is? Do you know that God's favour has the power to propel you to your breakthrough? Do you realize that His favour can re-structure systems and policies for your good?

Do you know that you are destined to walk in continuous flow of favour and operate from that realm? Do you know that a heart of worship is integral to receiving and enjoying the uncommon favour and blessings of our God?

God, in His mercy, has empowered me to write this book, **The Favour Dimension,** to enlighten you on the subject of divine favour, equip and propel you through it to fulfil your destiny, possess all your God-given inheritance, impact your generation, reign in life, and at the same time, be well-pleasing to Him.

Get yourself ready for a life-transforming journey through this book, and do let me hear from you of the glorious outcomes you receive from the revelations in this anointed kingdom resource—**The Favour Dimension.**

Apostle Ifeoma R. Fiiriter.

April 2018

CHAPTER 1

UNDERSTANDING FAVOUR

*N*ow, **what is favour you may ask, and how do we get it?** According to the All Nations English Dictionary (1990), Favour means "an act of kindness; approval; goodwill; to be in agreement with; to approve a plan or idea to one's advantage", etc.

Favour is also a reflection of something done to one's advantage. For example, Jesus Christ dying and shedding His blood on the cross for our redemption is a price paid to our advantage.

Vines Expository Dictionary Of Old & New Testament Words (1997, Thomas Nelson Publishers), defines favour as a mark of "being endowed with grace." Thus favour is closely linked with grace.

For me, favour is a grace gift from God. It is unmerited benevolence or blessing that God releases on individuals through any means He chooses at will. That implies that favour can be transferable. It can also be released on people by impartation through God's chosen servants.

Favour originates from God, and is rooted in His love. God is love (1 John 4:8). God pours out His favour upon people from the perspective of love, regardless of who they are, what they look like, where they are, using any means He chooses.

In this regard, you don't work to earn it. It is entirely

1

the preserve of God disbursed to whomever He deems fit. However, there are certain factors that can help trigger favour upon your life.

God can release favour directly on one's life or use somebody else to do it. Even when you receive favour from an individual, realize that it was God who touched their heart, softened it and moved them to favour you.

As you know, man in his natural state is selfish. Hence, the Bible tells us that "the tender mercies of the wicked *are* cruel" (Proverbs 12:10). The wicked in heart cannot genuinely favour anyone and neither will people easily do something good for another except God touches their heart to do so.

Thus, we must see and value every act of favour as coming from God directly or indirectly to us. Like other grace gifts of God, you just receive it as it is being poured out unto you and enjoy it. You will also need to discern its flow towards you daily, call it in, embrace it and maximize it to the glory of God.

Favour is a very strong force. It leaves indelible marks on its recipient, bringing blessings to them without adding any sorrow to it. Favour is a reliever. At all times, any act of favour will always bring relief and joy to the recipient.

David, at a very dismal time in his life, enjoyed tremendous favour from Jonathan, his covenant brother. That favour safeguarded David's life and ultimately brought him to a place where he could also favour Mephibosheth, Jonathan's son (2 Samuel 9:1-13).

Favour always leaves you with a smile and a 'wow!'

Favour helps you gain advantage over situations. It delivers into your hands something you may not necessarily qualify for. It leaves you with a state of holy wonder and awe to God, and gratitude to God, and the person whom God uses to bestow it.

Favour is positively contagious. **Laban** knew this first-hand from his association with Jacob, saying, "Please *stay*, if I have found favor in your eyes, *for* I have learned by experience that the LORD has blessed me for your sake" (Genesis 30:27).

Note: God is so interested to see us His children walk in His favour that He will not allow us to stay or settle in an environment of disfavour. He will find a way to get us to move from there to a better place. This He did for **Jacob**, and can also do for us.

We read:

> … Jacob saw the countenance of Laban, and indeed it *was* not *favorable* toward him as before. Then the LORD said to Jacob, "Return to the land of your fathers and to your family, and I will be with you … Then the Angel of God spoke to me in a dream, saying, 'Jacob.' And I said, 'Here I am.' And He said, 'Lift your eyes now and see, all the rams which leap on the flocks *are* streaked, speckled, and gray-spotted; for I have seen all that Laban is doing to you. I *am* the God of Bethel, where you anointed the pillar *and* where you made a vow to Me. Now arise, get out of this land,

and return to the land of your family.'" Then Jacob rose and set his sons and his wives on camels. And he carried away all his livestock and all his possessions which he had gained, his acquired livestock which he had gained in Padan Aram, to go to his father Isaac in the land of Canaan (Genesis 31:2-3, 11-13, 17-18).

Besides, God would not let Laban harm Jacob when he discovered the latter had fled his house with his family: " ... Laban was told on the third day that Jacob had fled. Then he took his brethren with him and pursued him for seven days' journey, and he overtook him in the mountains of Gilead. But God had come to Laban the Syrian in a dream by night, and said to him, "Be careful that you speak to Jacob neither good nor bad" (Genesis 31:22-24).

In the words of Jacob, "Thus I have been in your house twenty years; I served you fourteen years for your two daughters, and six years for your flock, and you have changed my wages ten times.

Unless the God of my father, the God of Abraham and the Fear of Isaac, had been with me, surely now you would have sent me away empty-handed. God has seen my affliction and the labor of my hands, and rebuked *you* last night" (Genesis 31:42).

Favour navigated Jacob's pathway back to his father's house, enabling him to overcome all challenges that came his way.

Still in connection with **favour by association,**

Potiphar and his household prospered exceedingly through his connection with Joseph (the favoured son of Jacob). We read, "The LORD was with Joseph, and he was a successful man; and he was in the house of his master the Egyptian. And his master saw that the LORD *was* with him and that the LORD made all he did to prosper in his hand" (Genesis 39:2-3).

Like a very strong and sweet fragrance, a tiny act of favour can have a very widespread impact on the recipient and others associated with them. Favour is like a long-awaited rainfall on a farmer's scorched ground, causing the seeds and crops planted to bud, grow well, get to full harvest stage, and ultimately bring happiness to the farmer.

Favour works to lift unnecessary pain or burden off of peoples' shoulders and bring comfort to them: "Blessed be the LORD, For He has shown His marvelous favor *and* lovingkindness to me [when I was assailed] in a besieged city" (Psalm 31:21, AMP).

Favour answers the deep pain and heart cries of people. Hence, one moment of favour has the capacity to wipe out a lifetime of sorrow, agony and failure in an instant. As a matter of fact, favour works to empower people for dominion lifestyle:

"LORD, by Your favor You have made my mountain stand strong; You hid Your face, *and* I was troubled … You have turned for me my mourning into dancing; You have put off my sackcloth and clothed me with gladness, To the end that *my* glory may sing praise to You and not be silent. O LORD my God, I will give thanks to You forever" (Psalm 30:7, 11-12). More on the benefits of favour later on in this book.

From the Bible, we see that God promised to favour His people, saying, "For I will look on you favorably and make you fruitful, multiply you and confirm My covenant with you" (Leviticus 26:9).

God poured out His favour on many people distinctly. For example, **Enoch,** a descendant of Seth, through God's favour escaped the natural order of death. He walked with God and God took him (Genesis 5:24).

Noah found favour with God (Genesis 6:8). **Abraham,** our father of faith (Romans 4:11), was bestowed with so much favour by God.

Thus, we read, " ... I will make you a great nation, And I will bless you [abundantly], And make your name great (exalted, distinguished); And you shall be a blessing [a source of great good to others] ... Now Abram was extremely rich in livestock and in silver and in gold" (Genesis 12:2; 13:2, AMP).

Notice, Abraham did not have to work for this before God bestowed it upon him. Abraham was already favoured and blessed by God even before he came into covenant with God i.e. before he became circumcised, a pointer to the righteousness of faith he had, which he was later going to pass on to his descendants (See Romans 4:9-12).

The **favour of God rested mightily on His chosen prophets to guarantee them total protection, deliverance, and provision in their times of need.**

When the prophet **Jeremiah** was cast into the

dungeon where there was no water but mire to die there, God showed him favour. He moved Ebed-Melech, an Ethiopian, one of the eunuchs in the king's palace, to go and appeal to the king to release Jeremiah from there, and he consented (See Jeremiah 38:4-13).

Thus, we read, "So they pulled Jeremiah up with ropes and lifted him out of the dungeon. And Jeremiah remained in the court of the prison" (Jeremiah 38:13).

At a time when the prophet **Elijah** was so discouraged in ministry and fled the nation for fear of Jezebel, while in the wilderness, under the broom tree, praying to die, God showed him favour and sent an angel there to go and feed him, giving him food and water that carried him for forty days and forty nights as far as Horeb, the mountain of God (See 1 Kings 19:3-8).

In **the new dispensation, favour comes to us through our Lord Jesus Christ**. I will share more on this in Chapter 4 of this book. Suffice it to say here that Jesus Christ, our Lord, understood the meaning and power of God's favour.

He connected the favour of God with the anointing of God. He saw favour as a divine enabling to get things done or make things happen supernaturally. **Jesus Christ centred His ministry on releasing the favour of God on peoples' lives.** To this effect, He set out to fulfil the prophetic word He received from Isaiah 61:1-3:

> The Spirit of the Lord God is upon me, Because the Lord has anointed *and* commissioned

me To bring good news to the humble *and* afflicted; He has sent me to bind up [the wounds of] the brokenhearted, To proclaim release [from confinement and condemnation] to the [physical and spiritual] captives And freedom to prisoners, To proclaim the favorable year of the LORD, And the day of vengeance *and* retribution of our God, To comfort all who mourn, To grant to those who mourn in Zion *the following*: To give them a turban instead of dust [on their heads, a sign of mourning], The oil of joy instead of mourning, The garment [expressive] of praise instead of a disheartened spirit. So they will be called the trees of righteousness [strong and magnificent, distinguished for integrity, justice, and right standing with God], The planting of the LORD, that He may be glorified

I need to mention that **Philip,** the evangelist, **enjoyed the favour of supernatural transportation** after his ministry to the Ethiopian eunuch.

We read, " ... he commanded the chariot to stand still. And both Philip and the eunuch went down into the water, and he baptized him. Now when they came up out of the water, the Spirit of the Lord caught Philip away, so that the eunuch saw him no more; and he went on his way rejoicing. But Philip was found at Azotus. And passing through, he preached in all the cities till he came to Caesarea" (Acts 8:38-40). Awesome!

The apostle **Peter was delivered from prison and untimely death through an angelic intervention of released favour** (See Acts 12:1-11). It is vital to note that anywhere and anytime favour is manifested, it comes with a divine coating or undertone. And that is why it has the power to change lives or anything it comes in contact with for good.

Sometimes **favour is connected with walking in righteousness and being disposed to doing good.** In this regard, favour may be deserved or gained.

Thus, we read, "For You, O LORD, will bless the righteous; With favor You will surround him as *with* a shield" (Psalm 5:12); "He who diligently seeks good seeks favor *and* grace, But he who seeks evil, evil will come to him" (Proverbs 11:27, AMP); "A good *man* obtains favor from the LORD, But a man of wicked intentions He will condemn" (Proverbs 12:2).

Notice, it is the righteous, not the sinner, and the good man, not the wicked, that God promises to bestow favour upon or surround with the shield of favour. As a shield, favour will serve as a mighty weapon of defence to the righteous—a defence against anything the enemy will throw at them.

Thus, favour can serve as a weapon or covering of protection, success, healing, provision, prosperity, financial deliverance or security, joy, freedom, and promotion to the righteous.

Still in relation to righteousness, we discover that **Noah** found grace with God because "he was a just man, perfect in his generations. Noah walked with God" (Genesis 6:9).

Although Abraham received God's favour before coming into covenant with Him, I believe that favour increased more and more thereafter as he began to walk in the ways of the Lord. In fact, scripture affirms that God will bestow favour upon us if we walk in His covenant:

'If you walk in My statutes and keep My commandments, and perform them, then I will give you rain in its season, the land shall yield its produce, and the trees of the field shall yield their fruit. Your threshing shall last till the time of vintage, and the vintage shall last till the time of sowing; you shall eat your bread to the full, and dwell in your land safely. I will give peace in the land, and you shall lie down, and none will make *you* afraid; I will rid the land of evil beasts, and the sword will not go through your land. You will chase your enemies, and they shall fall by the sword before you. Five of you shall chase a hundred, and a hundred of you shall put ten thousand to flight; your enemies shall fall by the sword before you. 'For I will look on you favorably and make you fruitful, multiply you and confirm My covenant with you. You shall eat the old harvest, and clear out the old because of the new. I will set My tabernacle among you, and My soul shall not abhor you. I will walk among you and be your God, and you shall be My people. I *am* the LORD your God, who brought you out of the land of Egypt, that *you* should not be their slaves; I have broken the bands of your yoke and made you walk upright (Leviticus 26:3-13).

Other **exceptions to favour being deserved or directly linked with righteousness** include those moments when God chooses to pour His rain on both the just and the wicked, and when He allows the sun to shine on both without discrimination (Matthew 5:45).

Let me observe that God does not grant favour to the wicked if their intention is to harm or kill His children. Hence, He preserved Paul from many demonic plots against his life.

We read, "Then the high priest and the chief men of the Jews informed him against Paul; and they petitioned him, asking a favor against him, that he would summon him to Jerusalem—while *they* lay in ambush along the road to kill him. But Festus answered that Paul should be kept at Caesarea, and that he himself was going *there* shortly" (Acts 2:2-4).

Of course, God's favour is graciously extended to the wicked or sinner at their point of repentance to save and bring them into His kingdom and subsequently enlist them to active service on earth:

For the [remarkable, undeserved] grace of

God that brings salvation has appeared to all men. It teaches us to reject ungodliness and worldly (immoral) desires, and to live sensible, upright, and godly lives [lives with a purpose that reflect spiritual maturity] in this present age, awaiting *and* confidently expecting the [fulfillment of our] blessed hope and the glorious appearing of our great God and Savior, Christ Jesus, who [willingly] gave Himself [to be crucified] on our behalf to redeem us *and* purchase our freedom from all wickedness, and to purify for Himself a chosen *and* very special people to be His own possession, *who are* enthusiastic for doing what is good (Titus 2:11-14, AMP).

Favour is not necessarily linked with work because it originates from God.

However, He calls us to daily approach His throne of grace to obtain the favour and mercy we need for each new day: "Therefore let us [with privilege] approach the throne of grace [that is, the throne of God's gracious favor] with confidence *and* without fear, so that we may receive mercy [for our failures] and find [His amazing] grace to help in time of need [an appropriate blessing, coming just at the right moment]" (Hebrews 4:16, AMP).

Thus, **prayer is a major favour trigger.** Through prayer, we get God to favourably intervene on our behalf when we face challenges in life. From scripture, we discover that the sons of Reuben and their team maximized this truth to win a battle that faced them.

We read, "The sons of Reuben, the Gadites, and half the tribe of Manasseh *had* forty-four thousand seven hundred and sixty valiant men, men able to bear shield and sword, to shoot with the bow, and skillful in war, who went to war.

They made war with the Hagrites, Jetur, Naphish, and Nodab. And they were helped against them, and the Hagrites were delivered into their hand, and all who *were* with them, for they cried out to God in the battle. He heeded their prayer, because they put their trust in Him.

Then they took away their livestock—fifty thousand of their camels, two hundred and fifty thousand of their sheep, and two thousand of their donkeys—also one hundred thousand of their men; for many fell dead, because the war *was* God's. And they dwelt in their place until the captivity" (1 Chronicles 5:18-22).

I need to stress that God often lavishes His favour on people who will come and put their trust in Him as evident in the text you just read.

Know that God intentionally releases His favour upon our lives so we can receive and enjoy it all our lifetime: "Sing praise to the LORD, you saints of His, And give thanks at the remembrance of His holy name. For His anger *is but for* a moment, His favor *is for* life; Weeping may endure for a night, But joy *comes* in the morning" (Psalm 30:4-5).

Also, realize that God wants us, having received

favour, to sow favour into other peoples' lives intentionally too. That way, we keep the stream of favour flowing in and through our lives for good.

For example, **Dorcas** was a New Testament believer in the early church who loved God and spent her time and resources to favour other people. Later on, at her time of need, she received favour in return, resulting in her being raised from the dead by the apostle Peter after prayer (See Acts 9:36-42).

May I reiterate that we receive God's favour through His sovereign will born out of love for us. So, although we can never buy God's favour, **certain factors can trigger or enhance the flow of God's favour into one's life**. I noted **walking in righteousness and prayer** earlier on.

And now I want to add **walking in love. O**ur love walk with God i.e. our cultivating and developing intimate relationship with Him—evidenced in our daily acts of intimate and pure worship of God, the quality of our word study and obedience to His word, our prayer lives, the use of our time and resources, etc., can open the door of favour unto us and also enhance the level of favour we walk in.

May I also say that **favour comes to us through the anointing we receive as we fellowship with God.** The more we do so, the more we increase in His anointing of favour and are also able to impart it to others too.

From **infancy, Jesus maintained a very close walk with the Father.** Thus, it is not surprising to read from Scripture that "Jesus increased in wisdom and stature, and in favor with God and men" (Luke 2:52);

" ... God anointed Jesus of Nazareth with the Holy Spirit and with great power; and He went around doing good and healing all who were oppressed by the devil, because God was with Him" (Acts 10:38, AMP).

I need to observe that the **covenant package of favour contained in Deuteronomy 28:1-13** is predicated on our walking closely with God and in obedience to His word.

Part of that package includes, "The LORD will open to you His good treasure, the heavens, to give the rain to your land in its season, and to bless all the work of your hand. You shall lend to many nations, but you shall not borrow. And the LORD will make you the head and not the tail; you shall be above only, and not be beneath, if you heed the commandments of the LORD your God, which I command you today, and are careful to observe *them"* (Deuteronomy 28:12-13).

Let me stress that all of God's plans for mankind and His acts are motivated by love—the root of favour. Think about the creation of the world, the supernatural healings, deliverances, and provisions He has released upon His people over the years.

In fact, the conception and birth of our Lord Jesus Christ, the Saviour of the world, were tangible manifestations of God's favour upon Mary, and for mankind at large. In the words of the angel Gabriel who brought the good news to Mary: "Rejoice, highly favored one, the Lord is with you; blessed are you among women!" (Luke 1:28). Always remember that

THE FAVOUR DIMENSION

God is the God of divine favour.

Jonah, the prophet, said this about God, "I know that You *are* a gracious and merciful God, slow to anger and abundant in lovingkindness, One who relents from doing harm" (Jonah 4:2).

God releases a measure of His divine favour on our lives each new day. Sometimes, this might not be very obvious and spectacular as we would expect. But it is still an evidence of God's favour poured out to us.

Examples include, waking us up in the morning to see a new day, protecting us from harm, healing or keeping us in perfect health, providing free parking lot for us when we desperately need one, and receiving pardon when we should have been fined or punished.

It also includes cancelling our debts, paying our way through college, receiving a grant or scholarship, having someone allow us to come into their lane on a busy road when we need that access, getting someone to give us a helping hand when we need it, and making us succeed in our chosen fields of endeavour—academics, ministry, business, home affairs, etc.

As a child of God, keep in mind that God wants to daily bestow His favour upon your life. Your present circumstances cannot hinder God bestowing His favour upon you.

Thus, you need to intentionally expect His favour to come upon your life each day, declare with your mouth that you are highly favoured of God, and His favour is yours now to receive and enjoy.

Scripture affirms: "For He says: "In an acceptable

time I have heard you, And in the day of salvation I have helped you." Behold, now *is* the accepted time; behold, now *is* the day of salvation ... His favor is for life; Weeping may endure for a night, But joy comes in the morning ... LORD, by Your favor You have made my mountain stand strong ...

For You, O LORD, will bless the righteous; With favor You will surround him as with a shield ... You will arise and have mercy on Zion; For the time to favor her, Yes, the set time, has come" (2 Corinthians 6:2; Psalm 30:5, 7; 5:12; 102:13).

Yes, this is your set time to receive and walk in God's favour. I prophesy over you right now that God will locate you with His covenant favour and through that re-locate you to your glorious covenant destiny in Jesus name. Receive that favour in Jesus name!

A Note Of Caution: We need to be careful not to abuse God's favour because it comes freely to us most of the time. We need to know that favour can be quenched or destroyed by pride and wilful sin against God.

King Nebuchadnezzar can teach us this priceless lesson. He was a king who was honoured by God with so much wealth and dominion. But at some point in his reign, his heart was lifted up with pride and sin, leading to his humiliation by God, after warning him through a dream interpreted by Daniel. We read:

> At the end of the twelve months he was walking about the royal palace of Babylon. The king

spoke, saying, "Is not this great Babylon, that I have built for a royal dwelling by my mighty power and for the honor of my majesty?" While the word *was still* in the king's mouth, a voice fell from heaven: "King Nebuchadnezzar, to you it is spoken: the kingdom has departed from you! And they shall drive you from men, and your dwelling *shall be* with the beasts of the field. They shall make you eat grass like oxen; and seven times shall pass over you, until you know that the Most High rules in the kingdom of men, and gives it to whomever He chooses." That very hour the word was fulfilled concerning Nebuchadnezzar; he was driven from men and ate grass like oxen; his body was wet with the dew of heaven till his hair had grown like eagles' *feathers* and his nails like birds' *claws* (Daniel 4:29-33).

Can you imagine a king of great honour suddenly being dethroned and reduced to the level where he was driven away by force to go and live in the forest with wild animals, and also eat like them? Ridiculous!

However, when Nebuchadnezzar humbled himself and recognized that he wasn't God, could not play God either, and that God alone is the Ruler of all the nations, he repented before God of his wicked ways, and began to praise and honour God publicly.

Consequently, God's favour came upon him and restored him fully back to his throne without any loss.

In his own words:

> And at the end of the time I, Nebuchadnezzar,
> lifted my eyes to heaven, and my understanding
> returned to me; and I blessed the Most High and
> praised and honored Him who lives forever: For
> His dominion *is* an everlasting dominion, And
> His kingdom *is* from generation to generation.
> All the inhabitants of the earth *are* reputed as
> nothing; He does according to His will in the
> army of heaven And *among* the inhabitants of
> the earth. No one can restrain His hand Or say
> to Him, "What have You done?" At the same
> time my reason returned to me, and for the
> glory of my kingdom, my honor and splendor
> returned to me. My counselors and nobles
> resorted to me, I was restored to my kingdom,
> and excellent majesty was added to me. Now
> I, Nebuchadnezzar, praise and extol and honor
> the King of heaven, all of whose works *are* truth,
> and His ways justice. And those who walk in
> pride He is able to put down (Daniel 4:34-37).

From Nebuchadnezzar's story, let's purposefully root
out all favour inhibitors and focus on practicing virtues
that trigger and sustain favour inflow into our lives.

THE FAVOUR DIMENSION

CHAPTER 2

WHEN ALL YOU NEED IS FAVOUR

*L*et me ask, have you experienced those moments in your life when you have tried so hard on working on something—a project, job, business, relationship, etc., to no avail? Presently, do you feel trapped in sorrow?

Do you feel weighed down by pressures of life? Do you feel discouraged? Do you feel as if nothing has changed in spite of all your prayers and sacrificial giving? Do you feel a sense of hopelessness and a very strong urge to throw in the towel and quit on God?

Are you battling prolonged illnesses that seem to have defied medical solution? Are you financially or emotionally stranded? Do you feel trapped in a hell-hole and need to escape and fly out on eagle's wings?

Perhaps, you have prayed and waited on God for many years to fulfil certain dreams on your heart and it looks impossible. In moments like these, **when you know that you have done all you need to do, and still have not got a breakthrough, all you need is God's favour.**

Thus, your prayer should be, "Yes, Lord, bring it on! Unleash Your rain of supernatural favour on my life! I vow in advance to give You the glory for all that

21

THE FAVOUR DIMENSION

You will do for me through your favour."

The Lord revealed to me a while ago in a vision that His favour will literally deliver our inheritances into our hands, fight our battles truly for us in every way and give us resounding victory and dominion over all enemies that have warred against our destinies.

Daily, I expect the greatest wave of God's supernatural favour to overwhelm and dominate my life and all that pertains to me. You too, should expect it, assured that our God is able. Thus says the Lord to you:

> ... My grace is sufficient for you [My lovingkindness and My mercy are more than enough—always available—regardless of the situation]; for [My] power is being perfected [and is completed and shows itself most effectively] in [your] weakness." Therefore, I will all the more gladly boast in my weaknesses, so that the power of Christ [may completely enfold me and] may dwell in me... It shall come to pass in that day That his burden will be taken away from your shoulder, And his yoke from your neck, And the yoke will be destroyed because of the anointing oil (2 Corinthians 12:9, AMP; Isaiah 10:27).

Yes, that's the anointing of favour referred to in that text you just read. It is the anointing that can shatter every yoke of bondage on a person's life and release

God's goodness upon them.

Also, know that God's grace i.e. His supernatural enabling or favour to help you overcome sin and all other afflictions or adversities of life, is available to you. God's strength, power, anointing and wisdom to live life skilfully and victoriously are available to you.

You can access them daily and freely by approaching the throne of grace: "And God is able to make all grace [every favor and earthly blessing] come in abundance to you, so that you may always [under all circumstances, regardless of the need] have complete sufficiency in everything [being completely self-sufficient in Him], and have an abundance for every good work *and* act of charity" (2 Corinthians 9:8, AMP).

So, intentionally maximize the divine injunction to daily approach the throne of grace (Hebrews 4:16), and do it with conviction. There lies the power to overcome life's school of hard-knocks:

"This is the word of the LORD to Zerubbabel: 'Not by might nor by power, but by My Spirit,' Says the LORD of hosts. 'Who are you, O great mountain? Before Zerubbabel you shall become a plain! And he shall bring forth the capstone With shouts of "Grace, grace to it!" (Zechariah 4:6-7). Remember, God shows no partiality (Acts 10:34). He is the same yesterday, today and forever (Hebrews 13:8).

God's grace or favour tackles your needs, including every emotional, health, financial, marital, and physical needs: "For you are recognizing [more clearly] the grace of our Lord Jesus Christ [His astonishing kindness, His generosity, His gracious favor], that though He was rich, yet for your sake He became poor, so that by His poverty you might become rich (abundantly blessed)" (2 Corinthians 8:9, AMP).

God has promised to not withhold any good thing from us His children: "For the LORD God *is* a sun and shield; The LORD will give grace and glory; No good *thing* will He withhold From those who walk uprightly" (Psalm 84:11).

Thus, I pray for you, if you are a child of God, that the favour of God will profusely abound to you. May His indwelling Holy Spirit within you release favour upon you to enable you take down every mountain of opposition before you and take hold of your breakthrough in Jesus name.

All hope is not lost. God is on your side. His favour is available to you—to answer every need in your life. Receive it now in Jesus name! His power to overcome is on your side. If God be for you, who can be against you? (Romans 8:31).

Let "The grace of the Lord Jesus Christ, and the love of God, and the communion of the Holy Spirit be with you ... Amen" (2 Corinthians 13:14).

CHAPTER 3

BIBLICAL MODELS TRANSFORMED BY GOD'S FAVOUR

*A*ll through the Bible, we read of the accounts of ordinary people who were radically transformed to uncommon heights of influence, success and victory through God's favour.

Examples include **Noah, Abraham, Joseph, Daniel, Ruth, Rahab, Esther, and Mephibosheth.** We are going to consider these now.

NOAH

Noah lived in an ungodly age with ungodly people. However, because he walked righteously before God, he found "favor *and* grace in the eyes of the LORD" (Genesis 6:8, AMP).

Through God's favour, Noah was spared from being judged along with the people of his day. God specifically gave him a plan to build an ark and enter into it with all his family and the animals and birds God told him to take along with him.

God empowered Noah, through His favour, to build that ark amidst the mockery of the people of his generation. Through following that plan, God ensured that Noah, his family, animals and birds in the ark were preserved from harm all through the period the flood waters of God's judgement covered the land.

Sequel to the clean offering Noah offered to God after he released him out of the ark, God cut a strong covenant of favour with Noah in which He blessed him tremendously. We read:

> Then Noah built an altar to the LORD, and took of every clean animal and of every clean bird, and offered burnt offerings on the altar. And the LORD smelled a soothing aroma. Then the LORD said in His heart, "I will never again curse the ground for man's sake, although the imagination of man's heart *is* evil from his youth; nor will I again destroy every living thing as I have done. "While the earth remains, Seedtime and harvest, Cold and heat, Winter and summer, And day and night Shall not cease" (Genesis 8:20-22).

In **chapter 3** of my book, **Unlimited Power Of The Seed,** I share profound revelation about Noah's seedtime and harvest experience. I encourage you to get the book and read the **5** amazing blessings God released upon Noah following from his planting his seed.

Meantime, let me insert an excerpt from **page 57 of the book** here for you: "God inhaled Noah's offering as a sweet smelling aroma. It was pleasing and acceptable to the Lord. Next, God took a decision to reverse the curse upon the land just because someone showed his love for God by giving a significant free-will offering.

This goes to show that our timely and qualitative offerings can actually work to bring deliverance to us, our families, communities, cities, and nations when sown with the right spirit to the Lord. Notice that Noah did not ask God for this miracle.

Nevertheless, God did it. Just as God reversed the curse upon a land back then through a man's offering, so much more can He do now for any child of God in obedience to God.

Indeed, there is no limit to the kind of blessings that God can pour out upon us through our offerings." **This just shows that our offerings can act as favour triggers.**

ABRAHAM

Abraham, as cited earlier on in this book, received the favour of God while an idol worshiper. He walked in it from the time God called him to leave his father's house to go the land He would show him (Genesis 12:1-2).

For the rest of his life, as he walked in righteousness, he enjoyed the favour of God and the tremendous blessing that came with it. For example, God prospered him exceedingly: "Abram *was* very rich in livestock, in silver, and in gold" (Genesis 13:2).

From **Genesis chapter 20:1-17,** we see that God

protected Abraham and Sarah from harm and danger all through their journey to the land God had for them. God would not even let King Abimelech touch Sarah even when Abraham, out of fear, lied, and gave her over to him (Genesis 20:6).

God so favoured Abraham that he even covered him when he sinned by lying to King Abimelech about Sarah, his wife, while on the other hand, God was prepared to destroy Abimelech for taking Sarah, Abraham's wife.

On top of that, God, without reprimanding Abraham, compelled Abimelech to restore Sarah back to Abraham with so much wealth and freedom to dwell in the land for as long as he wanted. He also answered Abraham's intercessory prayer for King Abimelech. This is where **favour seems to have a biased twist to it.**

Thus, we read: "Then Abimelech took sheep, oxen, and male and female servants, and gave *them* to Abraham; and he restored Sarah his wife to him. And Abimelech said, "See, my land *is* before you; dwell where it pleases you."

Then to Sarah he said, "Behold, I have given your brother a thousand *pieces* of silver; indeed this vindicates you before all who *are* with you and before everybody." Thus she was rebuked.

So Abraham prayed to God; and God healed Abimelech, his wife, and his female servants. Then they bore *children;* for the LORD had closed up all the wombs of the house of Abimelech because of Sarah, Abraham's wife" (Genesis 20:14-18).

Of course, **through favour, Abraham and Sarah received the much awaited child of promise, Isaac,** when they were fully advanced in age:

> For the promise that he would be the heir of the world *was* not to Abraham or to his seed through the law, but through the righteousness of faith. For if those who are of the law *are* heirs, faith is made void and the promise made of no effect, because the law brings about wrath; for where there is no law *there is* no transgression. Therefore *it is* of faith that *it might be* according to grace, so that the promise might be sure to all the seed, not only to those who are of the law, but also to those who are of the faith of Abraham, who is the father of us all (as it is written, "I have made you a father of many nations") in the presence of Him whom he believed—God, who gives life to the dead and calls those things which do not exist as though they did; who, contrary to hope, in hope believed, so that he became the father of many nations, according to what was spoken, "So shall your descendants be." And not being weak in faith, he did not consider his own body, already dead (since he was about a hundred years old), and the deadness of Sarah's womb. He did not waver at the promise of God through unbelief, but was strengthened in faith, giving

glory to God, and being fully convinced that what He had promised He was also able to perform. And therefore "it was accounted to him for righteousness" (Romans 4:13-22).

Bear in mind that, if you are a believer, you are a seed of Abraham and qualify to receive and enjoy the kind of favour he had: "And if you *are* Christ's, then you are Abraham's seed, and heirs according to the promise" (Galatians 3:29). God is not a respecter of persons. He can protect, bless, prosper and promote you as He did for Abraham.

JOSEPH

Joseph's unique story as the favoured child of his father unfolded when he was 17 years of age.

From the Book of Genesis chapter 37, we see that his father, Jacob, favoured him above his other siblings. Among other things, he made Joseph a coat of many colours, and that infuriated his brothers, who later on through a culmination of other factors sold him into slavery to some Ishmaelite traders, en-route to Egypt.

Joseph came into Egypt, not by choice, but by force through the sinister plot of his brothers. Joseph walked in remarkable wisdom. He was noted for honouring and fearing God, and ordering his steps accordingly.

As a result, God was with him throughout all the traumatic ordeals that he faced, helping him to overcome all of them, and subsequently exalting him in life. In Egypt, Joseph went through many experiences (some very challenging) that were overturned simply and totally by the favour of God on his life.

While in Potiphar's house, we read, "The LORD was with Joseph, and he was a successful man; and he was in the house of his master the Egyptian. And his master saw that the LORD *was* with him and that the LORD made all he did to prosper in his hand. So Joseph found favor in his sight, and served him. Then he made him overseer of his house, and all *that* he had he put under his authority.

So it was, from the time *that* he had made him overseer of his house and all that he had, that the LORD blessed the Egyptian's house for Joseph's sake; and the blessing of the LORD was on all that he had in the house and in the field. Thus he left all that he had in Joseph's hand, and he did not know what he had except for the bread which he ate" (Genesis 39:2-6).

Notice, it was the favour of God that made Joseph successful and prosperous while in Potiphar's house. It brought blessing on Joseph and Potiphar's house, including all that he had in the house and in the field (Genesis 39:5).

God's favour also elevated Joseph from being a slave to being the overseer of Potiphar's house, so much so that he "left all that he had in Joseph's hand, and he did not know what he had except for the bread which he ate" (Genesis 39:6).

When Joseph was sent into prison through the malicious plot of Potiphar's wife, God was still with him and showed him so much favour there:

"Then Joseph's master took him and put him into the prison, a place where the king's prisoners *were* confined. And he was there in the prison. But the LORD was with Joseph and showed him mercy, and He gave him favor in the sight of the keeper of the prison.

And the keeper of the prison committed to Joseph's hand all the prisoners who *were* in the prison; whatever they did there, it was his doing. The keeper of the prison did not look into anything *that was* under *Joseph's* authority, because the LORD was with him; and whatever he did, the LORD made *it* prosper" (Genesis 39:20-23).

Again, there in the prison, in the most unusual place and time, God gave Joseph favour in the sight of the keeper of the prison, who then committed all the rest of the prisoners in that prison into Joseph's care. Amazing!

Favour lifted Joseph up and made him take control of the prison to the glory of God. Favour created opportunities for Joseph to wisely use his God-given gifts of integrity, wisdom, service, and dream interpretation to serve people in need right there in the prison (See Genesis 40:1-20).

Although Joseph seemed to have been forgotten thereafter by the butler, whose dream he correctly interpreted, at the right time in God's plan, the same butler mentioned Joseph's name to Pharaoh who needed help understanding his own dream.

Through God's favour, Pharaoh was moved to bring Joseph quickly out of the dungeon or prison: "Then

Pharaoh sent and called Joseph, and they brought him quickly out of the dungeon; and he shaved, changed his clothing, and came to Pharaoh" (Genesis 41:14).

Let me reiterate that Joseph walked in remarkable wisdom, honouring and fearing God, and ordering his steps accordingly. As a result, God was with him throughout all the traumatic ordeals that he faced, helping him to overcome all of them.

On that set day, through God's divine intervention, Joseph's gifts made room for him. So although Joseph was dumped in the dungeon i.e. a strong underground prison cell, especially in a castle, to languish, as soon as Pharaoh, the king, had the need for the gift Joseph carried, without wasting time, he quickly sent for Joseph.

All his servants gave his command their utmost attention, stopped everything they were doing, went and hurriedly brought Joseph out of the dungeon. What a great relief that would have been for Joseph! And he took time to shave himself well, take a bath, and change his clothes before appearing to Pharaoh.

Once he appeared before Pharaoh, he never went back to the dungeon again, but up higher to the palace where he had been pre-designed by God to live and operate from.

Presently, I don't know what or which dungeon you have been dumped in by your haters. But I declare that this day, as you set your heart to please God like Joseph did against all odds, He will intervene to ensure that you are quickly brought out of that dungeon by someone with the power to do so for you in Jesus name.

Yes, God will apprehend or interrupt someone in a position to favour you to see and locate you and lift you up for good in Jesus name. Timely and right policies and procedures will be put in place to orchestrate your acceleration to your God-ordained place of significance and fulfilment in life. Receive God's favour for your deliverance and acceleration in Jesus name!

You are destined for the throne. Intentionally walk in the true fear of God, and He will cause His gifts deposited within you to make room for you and bring you before great people.

Remember, it was Joseph's gifts that directly brought him in contact with Pharaoh, the ruler of Egypt, whose dream he also accurately interpreted, and consequently advised him on what to do to safeguard his nation from the coming famine. We read:

> So the advice was good in the eyes of Pharaoh and in the eyes of all his servants. And Pharaoh said to his servants, "Can we find *such a one* as this, a man in whom *is* the Spirit of God?" Then Pharaoh said to Joseph, "Inasmuch as God has shown you all this, *there is* no one as discerning and wise as you. You shall be over my house, and all my people shall be ruled according to your word; only in regard to the throne will I be greater than you." And Pharaoh said to Joseph, "See, I have set you over all the land of Egypt." Then Pharaoh

took his signet ring off his hand and put it on Joseph's hand; and he clothed him in garments of fine linen and put a gold chain around his neck. And he had him ride in the second chariot which he had; and they cried out before him, "Bow the knee!" So he set him over all the land of Egypt. Pharaoh also said to Joseph, "I *am* Pharaoh, and without your consent no man may lift his hand or foot in all the land of Egypt (Genesis 41:37-44).

Notice, one moment of favour transformed Joseph's life for good. As I noted before, having come before Pharaoh, the favour of God kept him right there at the top of the national affairs of the nation of Egypt. Joseph wielded so much influence in the land.

Stephen, the evangelist, accurately sums up Joseph's story through these words, "... the patriarchs, becoming envious, sold Joseph into Egypt. But God was with him and delivered him out of all his troubles, and gave him favor and wisdom in the presence of Pharaoh, king of Egypt; and he made him governor over Egypt and all his house" (Acts 7:9-10).

Through his influential position, Joseph brought his father, his brothers, and their families to come and live with him in the land of Egypt, and situated them in the best place—Goshen. Thus, Joseph saved them from suffering during the years of famine in the land.

Know that one moment of God's favour can cancel out a lifetime of sorrow. I need to stress that Joseph walked in integrity and wisdom, and that greatly culminated in God's favour distinguishing him in life. If we want what Joseph had and enjoyed, we too, should be prepared to do what he did, even when it is costly to do so.

It is vital to mention that because favour is transgenerational, the favour on Joseph's life was passed down to his descendants. Thus, when Moses was pronouncing a blessing on the twelve tribes of Israel he released overwhelming measure of favour on the tribe of Joseph. In his words:

> ... of Joseph he said: "Blessed of the LORD *is* his land, With the precious things of heaven, with the dew, And the deep lying beneath, With the precious fruits of the sun, With the precious produce of the months, With the best things of the ancient mountains, With the precious things of the everlasting hills, With the precious things of the earth and its fullness, And the favor of Him who dwelt in the bush. Let *the blessing* come 'on the head of Joseph, And on the crown of the head of him *who was* separate from his brothers.' His glory *is like* a firstborn bull, And his horns *like* the horns of the wild ox; Together with them He shall push the peoples To the ends of the earth; They *are* the ten thousands of Ephraim, And they *are* the thousands of Manasseh (Deuteronomy 33:13-17).

Now let's move on to Daniel.

DANIEL

Daniel was taken into Babylon as a slave. There, he and his Hebrews companions, Hananiah (Shadrach), Mishael (Meshach), and Azariah (Abed-Nego), were among the young men chosen to receive adequate training and subsequent deployment to serve in the king's palace.

From the onset, "Daniel purposed in his heart that he would not defile himself with the portion of the king's delicacies, nor with the wine which he drank; therefore he requested of the chief of the eunuchs that he might not defile himself. Now God had brought Daniel into the favor and goodwill of the chief of the eunuchs" (Daniel 1:8-9).

Through favour, Daniel was granted a privilege others did not have. He was exempted from eating the king's delicacies which most likely would have been dedicated to their idols. In fact, when the chief of the eunuchs expressed his fear to Daniel about his decision, Daniel, through wisdom, requested him to test them for ten days.

We read, "Please test your servants for ten days, and let them give us vegetables to eat and water to drink. Then let our appearance be examined before you, and the appearance of the young men who eat the portion of the king's delicacies; and as you see fit, *so* deal with your servants."

So he consented with them in this matter, and tested them ten days. And at the end of ten days their features appeared better and fatter in flesh than all the young men who ate the portion of the king's delicacies. Thus the steward took away their portion of delicacies and the wine that they were to drink, and gave them vegetables" (Daniel 1:12-16).

Through favour, Daniel got King Nebuchadnezzar to grant him and his companions more time to tell him the interpretation of his dream. Also, God favoured Daniel and his companions when they sought him in prayer with the answer to Nebuchadnezzar's dream.

Consequently, Daniel was able to accurately tell and interpret the king's dream. That act swung open other doors of favour before Daniel and his companions: "Then the king promoted Daniel and gave him many great gifts; and he made him ruler over the whole province of Babylon, and chief administrator over all the wise *men* of Babylon.

Also Daniel petitioned the king, and he set Shadrach, Meshach, and Abed-Nego over the affairs of the province of Babylon; but Daniel *sat* in the gate of the king" (Daniel 2:48-49).

Let me add that the favour of God rested so much on Daniel and made him to serve prominently under the regimes of subsequent rulers of Babylon. In fact, in the time of King Belshazzar, God's favour brought Daniel into the limelight where his gift of dream interpretation was once again acknowledged and utilized to accurately read and interpret the writing on the wall that God sent to haunt the king.

As a result, "Belshazzar gave the command, and they clothed Daniel with purple and *put* a chain of gold around his neck, and made a proclamation concerning him that he should be the third ruler in the kingdom" (Daniel 5:29).

Even in the lion's den, God's favour was still on Daniel to protect him by shutting the mouths of the lions so that they did not harm him. He came out of the lion's den without injury to the amazement of all. Favour also vindicated him, made the king to honour the God of Daniel, the Most High God, and Daniel himself. Scripture reveals:

> And the king gave the command, and they brought those men who had accused Daniel, and they cast *them* into the den of lions— them, their children, and their wives; and the lions overpowered them, and broke all their bones in pieces before they ever came to the bottom of the den. Then King Darius wrote: To all peoples, nations, and languages that dwell in all the earth: Peace be multiplied to you. I make a decree that in every dominion of my kingdom *men must* tremble and fear before the God of Daniel. For He *is* the living God, And steadfast forever; His kingdom *is the one* which shall not be destroyed, And His dominion *shall endure* to the end. He delivers and rescues, And He works

signs and wonders In heaven and on earth, Who has delivered Daniel from the power of the lions. So this Daniel prospered in the reign of Darius and in the reign of Cyrus the Persian (Daniel 6:24-28). Notice, favour brought Daniel promotion, took him to the peak of his career with added longevity— from slave to Prime Minister of the nation.

RAHAB

Rahab was a gentile prostitute before she came in contact with the God of Israel. She risked her life to lodge the spies who Joshua, the Israeli army commander back then, sent to spy out the land of Jericho.

She revealed to them how much of a terror they were to her people because of the greatness of their God, and the certainty that God had given them the land of Jericho. In wisdom, she requested a fair token from them for lodging them. She literally asked them to favour her.

Consequently, she cut a covenant with them. Here is a part of their dialogue: "Now therefore, I beg you, swear to me by the LORD, since I have shown you kindness, that you also will show kindness to my father's house, and give me a true token, and spare my father, my mother, my brothers, my sisters, and all that they have, and deliver our lives from death."

So the men answered her, "Our lives for yours, if

none of you tell this business of ours. And it shall be, when the LORD has given us the land, that we will deal kindly and truly with you ... "According to your words, so *be* it." And she sent them away, and they departed. And she bound the scarlet cord in the window" (Joshua 2:12-14, 21).

As agreed, Rahab and her entire family were spared from destruction when the Israeli army came to destroy Jericho (Joshua 6:22-24).

In fact, we read, "And Joshua spared Rahab the harlot, her father's household, and all that she had. So she dwells in Israel to this day, because she hid the messengers whom Joshua sent to spy out Jericho" (Joshua 6:25).

Through favour, Rahab was adopted into the Jewish family and given citizenship there. In addition, she later became the great grand-mother of David, through whose lineage our Lord Jesus Christ came: "The book of the genealogy of Jesus Christ, the Son of David, the Son of Abraham ... Salmon begot Boaz by Rahab, Boaz begot Obed by Ruth, Obed begot Jesse, and Jesse begot David the king" (Matthew 1:1, 5-6).

Favour lifted Rahab out of a deplorable lifestyle to a glorious and dignifying one.

RUTH

Ruth was another gentile woman favoured by God. She was the daughter-in-law of Rahab (Matthew 1:5). She left her native land, Moab, amidst great loss of her first husband, her father-in-law, and her brother-in-law.

She rejected the plea of Naomi, her mother-in-law, to remain in the land of Moab after the loss of her husband, and rather chose to return with her to Bethlehem, Judah.

She and Naomi came into the land of Judah broke, but through favour their lives were totally transformed. From the onset, Ruth, through Naomi's permission and support, went out to glean heads of grain in the field of Boaz, a wealthy land-proprietor.

There, the favour of God overtook her. As soon as Boaz came into the field that day, he noticed her and made enquiries about her. He further spoke to her personally:

"Then Boaz said to Ruth, "You will listen, my daughter, will you not? Do not go to glean in another field, nor go from here, but stay close by my young women. *Let* your eyes *be* on the field which they reap, and go after them. Have I not commanded the young men not to touch you? And when you are thirsty, go to the vessels and drink from what the young men have drawn."

So she fell on her face, bowed down to the ground, and said to him, "Why have I found favor in your eyes, that you should take notice of me, since I *am* a foreigner?" (Ruth 2:8-10).

The favour of God prevailed upon her all through the harvest time, and later on culminated in her marriage to Boaz. Through that union, she was blessed with a son, Obed, "the father of Jesse, the father of David"

(Ruth 4:17).

Favour transformed both of Ruth's and Naomi's lives from pain, ugliness, deprivation, and sorrow, to one of honour, beauty, prosperity, fruitfulness, uncommon bliss, and fulfilment.

ESTHER

Esther was a Jewish orphan slave girl brought up by her cousin, Mordecai, in the Medo-Persia Empire of King Ahasuerus.

Through the king's command, Esther was among the beautiful young virgins brought into Shushan palace under the custody of Hagai, the king's eunuch. They were to undergo a one-year beauty treatment before being sent to the king to spend a night with him. This was for him to pick the one that suits him best as his new queen, after Vashti was removed.

Favour distinguished Esther over all her competitors. The Bible reveals that Esther found favour in the sight of all who saw her, including the king, who eventually chose her as his wife and queen, and also held a big party in her honour.

We read, "Now when the turn came for Esther the daughter of Abihail the uncle of Mordecai, who had taken her as his daughter, to go in to the king, she requested nothing but what Hegai the king's eunuch, the custodian of the women, advised.

And Esther obtained favor in the sight of all who saw her. So Esther was taken to King Ahasuerus, into his royal palace, in the tenth month, which *is* the month of Tebeth, in the seventh year of his reign.

The king loved Esther more than all the *other* women, and she obtained grace and favor in his sight more than all the virgins; so he set the royal crown upon her head and made her queen instead of Vashti.

Then the king made a great feast, the Feast of Esther, for all his officials and servants; and he proclaimed a holiday in the provinces and gave gifts according to the generosity of a king" (Esther 2:15-18).

It is crucial to note that Esther was highly favoured by her husband, the king. Favour preserved Esther life from untimely death that could have resulted for venturing to meet the king unsummoned.

After her three days fasting exercise along with her maids and the rest of the Jews in the palace, Esther went to approach the king and found favour before him: "So it was, when the king saw Queen Esther standing in the court, *that* she found favor in his sight, and the king held out to Esther the golden scepter that *was* in his hand.

Then Esther went near and touched the top of the scepter. And the king said to her, "What do you wish, Queen Esther? What *is* your request? It shall be given to you—up to half the kingdom!" (Esther 5:2-3).

The favour that was unleashed upon Esther by God after her fasting exercise sustained and empowered her to accomplish all her heart's desires for herself and her people.

She received so many favours from her husband, all

of which led to the destruction of Haman, the Jewish enemy, his entire family, and the advancement of Mordecai from being a gate keeper to becoming the Prime Minister of the nation.

Also, through favour, Esther and Mordecai got the king's approval to issue another letter signed in the king's name to revoke the letters devised by Haman to annihilate the Jews on a set date. That letter also empowered them to defend themselves against their adversaries on the day they were set to attack them (See Esther 8:1-17). As a result, the Jews, assisted by many of the king's officials, destroyed all their enemies (See Esther 9:1-15).

They also went on to celebrate their victory amidst great joy, thanksgiving and giving of gifts over two days: " ... the Jews who *were* at Shushan assembled together on the thirteenth *day,* as well as on the fourteenth; and on the fifteenth of *the month* they rested, and made it a day of feasting and gladness. Therefore the Jews of the villages who dwelt in the unwalled towns celebrated the fourteenth day of the month of Adar *with* gladness and feasting, as a holiday, and for sending presents to one another (Esther 9:18-19):

Notice that favour lifted Esther up from a nonentity to a queen, a woman of honour and uncommon influence in the king's Empire—whose legacy is still being celebrated today in Israel and across the world.

Also, that wind of favour that came upon her life positively affected Mordecai, advancing him to the position of Prime Minister of the Medo-Persian

Empire. Favour lifted both of them out of deprivation and servitude to glory and dominion lifestyle.

MEPHIBOSHETH

Mephibosheth was the son of Jonathan, David's bosom covenant brother. I have already shared so much on the covenant privileges Mephibosheth received from King David in my book, **"From Lodebar To The Palace: Maximizing The Power Of Divine Covenant."**

I encourage you to read that book, obtainable from our website, www.favourbooksandmusic.com OR FavourLandBooks on Amazon. Its Kindle version is available from Amazon.

Here is an amazing testimony about this book: "I want to say a big thanks to you for this wonderful book, "From Lo Debar To The Palace: Maximizing The Power Of Divine Covenant." It gave me the wonderful experience of the love of God"—G.J., P.H., Nigeria.

Meanwhile, suffice it to say here that favour totally rearranged Mephibosheth's life for good. He was favoured by King David because of the covenant that existed between his dad and David.

Although lame in his feet, and dwelling in Lo debar out of hardship, through favour, Mephibosheth was moved out of Lo Debar by King David into his palace, where he was also allowed to enjoy all the royal privileges accorded to the sons of David.

Through favour, Mephibosheth received double honour. From being and living as an ordinary citizen in Lo Debar—a place of total deprivation—he was elevated to a place of honour and distinction where he lived and dined with people of nobility.

Through favour, Mephibosheth was granted full restoration of the wealth of his grand-father, King Saul, and his father, Jonathan (See 2 Samuel 9.7). Mephibosheth had Ziba and his children till the land for him while he lived in the palace and fed sumptuously out of King David's table (2 Samuel 9:9-13).

Through favour, Mephibosheth was delivered from fear (2 Samuel 9:7). Through favour, he regained his true identity as someone of nobility. Also, he received supernatural promotion, provision, and protection without discrimination from King David (2 Samuel 9:11-13).

Like Mephibosheth, no matter where you are today or what your circumstances are, know that favour will bring you out from the pit to the top.

THE EARLY CHURCH

The early church was born under the wings of divine favour through the supernatural act of the Holy Spirit coming upon them on the day of Pentecost. (Acts 2:1-4).

This was in fulfilment of Jesus' promise to them: "Behold, I send the Promise of My Father upon you; but tarry in the city of Jerusalem until you are endued with power from on high ... But the Helper, the Holy Spirit, whom the Father will send in My name, He will teach you all things, and bring to your remembrance all things that I said to you" (Luke 24:49; John 14:25). We further read about the early church:

> And with many other words he testified and exhorted them, saying, "Be saved from this perverse generation." Then those who gladly received his word were baptized; and that day about three thousand souls were added *to them*. And they continued steadfastly in the apostles' doctrine and fellowship, in the breaking of bread, and in prayers. Then fear came upon every soul, and many wonders and signs were done through the apostles. Now all who believed were together, and had all things in common, and sold their possessions and goods, and divided them among all, as anyone had need. So continuing daily with one accord in the temple, and breaking bread from house to house, they ate their food with gladness and simplicity of heart, praising God and having favor with all the people. And the Lord added to the church daily those who were being saved … And with great power the apostles gave witness to the resurrection of the Lord Jesus. And great grace was upon them all. Nor was there anyone among them who lacked; for all who were possessors of lands or houses sold them, and brought the proceeds of the things that were sold, and laid *them* at

the apostles' feet; and they distributed to each
as anyone had need (Acts 2:40-47; 4:33-35).

Through God's favour they were empowered to preach
the word of God in power and turn their world upside
down to the glory of God: "These who have turned the
world upside down have come here too" (Acts 17).

What made them turn their world upside down?
The favour of God evolving from their total dependency
on the Holy Spirit—their gift of favour, who ushered
them into living and effectively operating from the
favour dimension.

Favour sustained and empowered them to still preach
the word of God after they were scattered everywhere
by persecution. Scripture affirms that "the hand of the
Lord was with them, and a great number believed and
turned to the Lord.

Then news of these things came to the ears of the
church in Jerusalem, and they sent out Barnabas to
go as far as Antioch. When he came and had seen the
grace of God, he was glad, and encouraged them all
that with purpose of heart they should continue with
the Lord" (Acts 11:21-23).

Favour made them multiply exceedingly and also
met their needs. All the outstanding miracles, signs
and wonders that characterized and distinguished their
ministry were tangible products of God's favour on
their lives.

In every place they found themselves, they spoke
"boldly in the Lord, who was bearing witness to the

word of His grace, granting signs and wonders to be done by their hands" (Acts 14:3).

Today, we still have access to that same Holy Spirit who rained down God's favour upon them. And we can receive as much as they did from the Holy Spirit or even more because there is no limit to what God can do.

Daily, His favour richly extends to us, beckoning us to come and receive it and use it to His glory. Hence, we are to "come boldly to the throne of grace, that we may obtain mercy and find grace to help in time of need" (Hebrews 4:16).

Through **favour, the early church overcame many obstacles in their way of service, received timely healing, deliverances, and protection.** Here is part of Paul's epistle to the Philippian believers about Epaphroditus:

" ... I considered it necessary to send to you Epaphroditus, my brother, fellow worker, and fellow soldier, but your messenger and the one who ministered to my need; since he was longing for you all, and was distressed because you had heard that he was sick.

For indeed he was sick almost unto death; but God had mercy on him, and not only on him but on me also, lest I should have sorrow upon sorrow. Therefore I sent him the more eagerly, that when you see him again you may rejoice, and I may be less sorrowful.

Receive him therefore in the Lord with all gladness, and hold such men in esteem; because for the work of Christ he came close to death, not regarding his life, to supply what was lacking in your service toward me (Philippians 2:25-30).

Notice, not only did Epaphroditus recover from sickness through God's favour, but Paul also wanted the brethren to fully rejoice and appreciate what God did for him when they saw him.

In addition, Paul wanted them to honour the man with more favour. No doubt, favour brings joy wherever it is released, and also triggers more favour.

PAUL

Last, but not the least, is the apostle Paul. Although Paul was part of the early church, I feel it is vital to single him out here and note the tremendous favour he walked in regardless of all the hazardous situations he often found himself in.

Many attempts were made by his enemies to kill him prematurely. But through God's favour Paul was delivered and preserved from harm. We read, "Now after many days were past, the Jews plotted to kill him. But their plot became known to Saul. And they watched the gates day and night, to kill him. Then the disciples took him by night and let *him* down through the wall in a large basket" (Acts 9:23-25).

After the Euroclydon shipwreck experience, the soldiers planned to kill all the prisoners, but favour intervened to save Paul's life and that of the other prisoners.

We read, " … the soldiers' plan was to kill the

prisoners, lest any of them should swim away and escape. But the centurion, wanting to save Paul, kept them from *their* purpose, and commanded that those who could swim should jump *overboard* first and get to land, and the rest, some on boards and some on *parts* of the ship. And so it was that they all escaped safely to land" (Acts 27:42-44).

While in his defence before King Agrippa, Paul stated, " ... King Agrippa, I was not disobedient to the heavenly vision, but declared first to those in Damascus and in Jerusalem, and throughout all the region of Judea, and *then* to the Gentiles, that they should repent, turn to God, and do works befitting repentance.

For these reasons the Jews seized me in the temple and tried to kill *me*. Therefore, having obtained help from God, to this day I stand, witnessing both to small and great" (Acts 26:19-22).

Even as a prisoner, Paul enjoyed freedom not given to others. In Sidon i.e. on his way to Rome, Paul received favour from the Roman centurion, Julius, who "treated Paul kindly and gave *him* liberty to go to his friends and receive care" (Acts 27:3).

In Rome, Paul "dwelt two whole years in his own rented house, and received all who came to him, preaching the kingdom of God and teaching the things which concern the Lord Jesus Christ with all confidence, no one forbidding him" (Acts 28:30-31). Favour empowered Paul to finish his race well and strong too, bringing God glory through it all.

CHAPTER 4

JESUS CHRIST, NEW COVENANT SOURCE OF FAVOUR

*A*s I stated earlier in this book, in the new dispensation, favour comes to us through our Lord Jesus Christ.

Favour is rooted in God's love echoed through a divine covenant He has made with us through the shed blood of Jesus:

> For the Law was given through Moses, but grace [the unearned, undeserved favor of God] and truth came through Jesus Christ ... In love He predestined *and* lovingly planned for us to be adopted to Himself as [His own] children through Jesus Christ, in accordance with the kind intention *and* good pleasure of His will— to the praise of His glorious grace *and* favor, which He so freely bestowed on us in the Beloved [His Son, Jesus Christ] ... and to Jesus, the Mediator of a new covenant [uniting God and man], and to the sprinkled blood, which speaks [of mercy], a better *and* nobler *and* more gracious message than *the blood* of Abel [which cried out for vengeance] (John

THE FAVOUR DIMENSION

1:17; Ephesians 1:5-6; Hebrews 12:24, AMP).

The **favour of God brought us salvation**: "But God, who is rich in mercy, because of His great love with which He loved us, even when we were dead in trespasses, made us alive together with Christ (by grace you have been saved), and raised *us* up together, and made *us* sit together in the heavenly *places* in Christ Jesus, that in the ages to come He might show the exceeding riches of His grace in *His* kindness toward us in Christ Jesus.

For by grace you have been saved through faith, and that not of yourselves; *it is* the gift of God, not of works, lest anyone should boast (Ephesians 2:4-9).

Jesus, during His final moments with His disciples, touched on the fact that redemption and the Holy Spirit would come through Him, saying, "Thus it is written, and thus it was necessary for the Christ to suffer and to rise from the dead the third day, and that repentance and remission of sins should be preached in His name to all nations, beginning at Jerusalem.

And you are witnesses of these things. Behold, I send the Promise of My Father upon you; but tarry in the city of Jerusalem until you are endued with power from on high" (Luke 24:46-49.

The apostle Paul further noted that Jesus Christ paid the price for our redemption: "For the grace of God that brings salvation has appeared to all men, teaching us that, denying ungodliness and worldly lusts, we should live soberly, righteously, and godly in the present age, looking for the blessed hope and glorious appearing of our great God and Savior Jesus Christ, who gave Himself for us, that He might redeem us from every lawless deed and purify for Himself *His* own special people, zealous for good works" (Titus 2:11-14).

As mentioned previously in this book, Jesus Christ, our Lord, understood the power of walking in God's favour. He read from the scroll of Isaiah, and carefully centred His earthly ministry on what He discovered from it.

In one of the Jewish synagogues, He read and declared publicly: "The Spirit of the Lord [is] upon Me, because He has anointed Me [the Anointed One, the Messiah] to preach the good news (the Gospel) to the poor;

He has sent Me to announce release to the captives and recovery of sight to the blind, to send forth as delivered those who are oppressed [who are downtrodden, bruised, crushed, and broken down by calamity], To proclaim the accepted and acceptable year of the Lord [the day when salvation and the free favors of God profusely abound" (Luke 4:18-19, AMP).

Having read and understood that, Jesus proceeded to focus His ministry on introducing the reign of God's favour into the troubled waters of peoples' lives. Hence, He healed the sick, set the captives free, made the dumb to speak, opened blind eyes, deaf ears, raised the dead, fed the hungry, met the needs of the poor, etc.

The Bible reveals this truth to us, saying, "... God

anointed Jesus of Nazareth with the Holy Spirit and with power, who went about doing good and healing all who were oppressed by the devil, for God was with Him ... For you know the grace of our Lord Jesus Christ, that though He was rich, yet for your sakes He became poor, that you through His poverty might become rich" (Acts 10:38; 2 Corinthians 8:9);

"Christ purchased our freedom [redeeming us] from the curse (doom) of the Law [and its condemnation] by [Himself] becoming a curse for us, for it is written [in the Scriptures], Cursed is everyone who hangs on a tree (is crucified); To the end that through [their receiving] Christ Jesus, the blessing [promised] to Abraham might come upon the Gentiles, so that we through faith might [all] receive [the realization of] the promise of the [Holy] Spirit" (Galatians 3:13-14, AMP).

It is vital to note that **the Holy Spirit is Jesus' blood Gift of favour to the believer to help preserve, nurture, and bless them in life and also instruct and equip them for effective service in God's kingdom.** Jesus affirmed:

It is to your advantage that I go away; for if I do not go away, the Helper will not come to you; but if I depart, I will send Him to you. And when He has come, He will convict the world of sin, and of righteousness, and of judgment: of sin, because they do not believe in Me; of righteousness, because I go to My Father and you see Me no more; of judgment, because the ruler of this world is judged. "I still have many things to say to you, but you cannot bear *them* now. However, when He, the Spirit of truth, has come, He will guide you into all truth; for He will not speak on His own *authority,* but whatever He hears He will speak; and He will tell you things to come. He will glorify Me, for He will take of what is Mine and declare *it* to you. All things that the Father has are Mine. Therefore I said that He will take of Mine and declare *it* to you … But the Helper, the Holy Spirit, whom the Father will send in My name, He will teach you all things, and bring to your remembrance all things that I said to you … Behold, I send the Promise of My Father upon you; but tarry in the city of Jerusalem until you are endued with power from on high … to Jesus the Mediator of the new covenant, and to the blood of sprinkling that speaks better things than *that of* Abel (John 16:7-15; 14:25; Luke 24:49; Hebrews 12:24).

The fulfilment of this promise was the Holy Spirit coming upon His bunch of fearful apostles and disciples on the day of Pentecost, baptizing them with the gift of speaking in tongues, and crowning them with so much favour, boldness, and power that enabled them to walk in dominion over all their enemies in the their day, and turn their world upside down to the glory of God (See previous notes on the early church in chapter 3 of this

THE FAVOUR DIMENSION

book).

CHAPTER 5

33 BENEFITS OF DIVINE FAVOUR

*D*ivine Favour has so many amazing and inestimable benefits. Although we have touched on some of these in previous chapters, we will consider these benefits in greater detail here.

1. Favour Eliminates Fear. When you hear or receive disturbing news, it brings with it some form of fear, anxiety or panic. Only God's intervention evidenced through favour can tackle this, and ultimately destroy the inherent potential fear in the news. Only favour can step in to dilute or quench the fear that can evolve from negative or disturbing news.

When Mary, the mother of our Lord Jesus Christ, received the strange angelic visitor and his troubling news to her, she became afraid. But the angel released a word of favour upon her that eliminated her fears, enabled her to take in the rest of the news, and prepare herself to play her role in accomplishing the plan of God.

We read, "But when she saw *him,* she was troubled at his saying, and considered what manner of greeting this was. Then the angel said to her, "Do not be afraid, Mary, for you have found favor with God. And behold, you will conceive in your womb and bring forth a Son, and shall call His name JESUS" (Luke 1:29-31).

2. Favour Is A Mark Of Divine Approval. It shows that you have been approved of God. You have been endowed with grace for your next assignment. You are placed in an advantaged position by God where He will shield you and help you fulfil His plans for your life.

This truth was encapsulated in the angel Gabriel's word to Mary, saying, "Do not be afraid, Mary, for you have found favor with God. And behold, you will conceive in your womb and bring forth a Son, and shall call His name JESUS" (Luke 1:30-31).

Also, at the baptism of Jesus Christ, God's open endorsement of Him was a mark of divine approval: "When all the people were baptized, it came to pass that Jesus also was baptized; and while He prayed, the heaven was opened. And the Holy Spirit descended in bodily form like a dove upon Him, and a voice came from heaven which said, "You are My beloved Son; in You I am well pleased" (Luke 3:21-22).

Bear in mind that Jesus' ministry was fully launched after this open affirmation from the Father.

3. Favour Delivers One From Harm's Way. I noted earlier on in this book that the favour of God rescued the prophet **Jeremiah** from the dungeon where he sank in the mire.

The favour of God preserved **Elijah** from starvation and sustained him during the famine in the land of Israel, and also when he fled the land into the wilderness because of Jezebel. **David,** the psalmist, understood this truth about favour delivering one from harm's way, and thus declared, "Blessed be the LORD, For He has shown His marvelous favor *and* lovingkindness to me [when I was assailed] in a besieged city" (Psalm 31:21, AMP).

The apostle **Paul** acknowledged that God's favour preserved him from harm: "For these reasons the Jews seized me in the temple and tried to kill *me*. Therefore, having obtained help from God, to this day I stand, witnessing both to small and great, saying no other things than those which the prophets and Moses said would come" (Acts 26:21-22; see also Acts 9:23-25).

4. Favour Makes One Rich Without Added Sorrow. Such was the case with Abraham. God blessed him with favour when He called him to leave his father's land to go to the land God had for him.

As a result of that favour, Abraham prospered greatly: "Now the LORD had said to Abram: "Get out of your country, From your family And from your father's house, To a land that I will show you. I will make you a great nation; I will bless you And make your name great; And you shall be a blessing … Abram *was* very rich in livestock, in silver, and in gold" (Genesis 12:1-2; 13:2).

5. Favour Brings Supernatural Fruitfulness And Dominion. Through God's favour coming upon Mary, she received grace to conceive and bring forth Jesus Christ, our Saviour, who had, and still has dominion over all things:

Then the angel said to her, "Do not be afraid, Mary, for you have found favor with God. And behold, you will conceive in your womb and bring forth a Son, and shall call His name JESUS. He will be great, and will be called the Son of the Highest; and the Lord God will give Him the throne of His father David. And He will reign over the house of Jacob forever, and of His kingdom there will be no end."

Then Mary said to the angel, "How can this be, since I do not know a man?" And the angel answered and said to her, "*The* Holy Spirit will come upon you, and the power of the Highest will overshadow you; therefore, also, that Holy One who is to be born will be called the Son of God" (Luke 2:30-35).

6. Favour Brings Supernatural Provision. Favour cancels out debt, lack, insufficiency and deprivation. Favour brought supernatural provision to the prophet **Elijah** at a time of severe drought and famine in the land. As a result, he was fed by the ravens at the Brook Cherith and subsequently by the widow of Zarephath (See 1 Kings 17:2-6, 13-16). Favour ensured that Elijah had no lack all the time the land was plagued by drought.

Paul received supernatural provision after his ministry in the Island of Malta at a critical time in his life: "They also honored us in many ways; and when we departed, they provided such things as were necessary" (Acts 28:10).

7. Favour Brings Supernatural Promotion. Favour brought promotion to people like Daniel, Shadrach, Meshach, and Abed-Nego, while in exile in Babylon. From being slaves, each of these men rose to very prominent positions in that nation.

8. Favour Brings Relief From Ministerial Burden.
Moses understood this truth, and thus cried out to the
Lord amidst his pain for a relief, saying:

"Why have You afflicted Your servant? And why
have I not found favor in Your sight, that You have laid
the burden of all these people on me? Did I conceive
all these people? Did I beget them, that You should
say to me, 'Carry them in your bosom, as a guardian
carries a nursing child,' to the land which You swore
to their fathers?

Where am I to get meat to give to all these people?
For they weep all over me, saying, 'Give us meat, that
we may eat.' I am not able to bear all these people
alone, because the burden *is* too heavy for me. If You
treat me like this, please kill me here and now—if I
have found favor in Your sight—and do not let me see
my wretchedness! (Numbers 11:11-15).

In answer to his cry, God showed up with a solution
of favour: "So the LORD said to Moses: "Gather to Me
seventy men of the elders of Israel, whom you know
to be the elders of the people and officers over them;
bring them to the tabernacle of meeting, that they may
stand there with you.

Then I will come down and talk with you there. I
will take of the Spirit that *is* upon you and will put
the same upon them; and they shall bear the burden of
the people with you, that you may not bear *it* yourself
alone" (Numbers 11:16-17).

From personal experience, I can honestly tell you

that the burdens God's servants face as they carry out their assignments can be so overwhelming that they daily need a dose of God's favour to surmount them.

9. Favour Fixes Broken Things And Broken Lives And Makes Them Shine to the Glory Of God. Think about how God's favour turned the lives of people like Joseph, Naomi, Ruth, David, Esther, Daniel, etc. around for His glory.

In the same way, favour will turn your life around from turmoil to rest and peace— get you out of debt, heal your body or your loved ones, bless your business, career, studies, etc.—whatever you do uprightly, regardless of where you are.

Regarding Naomi and Ruth, after the death of Naomi's husband and her two children in Moab, she was heart-broken and bitter in spirit. This so gravely impacted her that she changed her name to 'Mara,' which means 'bitter.'

But through favour, Ruth, her daughter-in-law, got married to Boaz, a wealthy land proprietor, through whom Ruth eventually had a son, Obed, subsequently nursed by Naomi. She was so full of joy following from that experience, and was also celebrated by the women of her day:

"Then the women said to Naomi, "Blessed *be* the LORD, who has not left you this day without a close relative; and may his name be famous in Israel! And may he be to you a restorer of life and a nourisher of your old age; for your daughter-in-law, who loves you, who is better to you than seven sons, has borne him."

Then Naomi took the child and laid him on her bosom, and became a nurse to him. Also the neighbor women gave him a name, saying, "There is a son born to Naomi." And they called his name Obed. He *is* the father of Jesse, the father of David" (See Ruth 4: 14-17).

Remember, Naomi was totally fixed and restored in life through favour, and that can be your portion too, if you need it.

10. Favour Lifts One From The Pit Into The Palace. Favour lifted Joseph out from the pit where he was dumped out of envy by his brothers (Genesis 37:21-23), and ultimately into the palace (Genesis 41:39-44). It lifted him to a position of power and influence where he was able to lay down certain landmarks that outlasted him.

11. Favour Empowers One To Reign In Life. As a child of God, realize that you are the righteousness of God in Christ Jesus, and His favour is available to you to enable you reign in this life: "For if by the one man's offense death reigned through the one, much more those who receive abundance of grace and of the gift of righteousness will reign in life through the One, Jesus Christ.)" (Romans 5:17).

12. Favour Brings Wealth Transfer. Before the Israelites left Egypt under Moses' leadership, God gave them remarkable favour before the Egyptians. That favour made them to plunder the latter.

We read: "So I will stretch out My hand and strike Egypt with all My wonders which I will do in its midst;

and after that he will let you go. And I will give this people favor in the sight of the Egyptians; and it shall be, when you go, that you shall not go empty-handed.

But every woman shall ask of her neighbor, namely, of her who dwells near her house, articles of silver, articles of gold, and clothing; and you shall put *them* on your sons and on your daughters. So you shall plunder the Egyptians ...

Now the children of Israel had done according to the word of Moses, and they had asked from the Egyptians articles of silver, articles of gold, and clothing. And the LORD had given the people favor in the sight of the Egyptians, so that they granted them *what they requested.* Thus they plundered the Egyptians (Exodus 3:20-22; 12:35-36).

13. Favour Brings Restoration. Favour restored the Shunammite woman's dead son back to life after the prophet Elisha prayed for him (See 2 Kings 4:32-37). On her return to Israel after a seven-year sojourn in the land of the Philistines, she went to the king to seek possession of her land.

Through favour, the king offered her total restoration of everything that was hers, including her land and the proceeds from it from the time of her departure until her return.

We read, "So the king appointed a certain officer for her, saying, "Restore all that *was* hers, and all the proceeds of the field from the day that she left the land until now" (2 Kings 8:6).

14. Favour Gives One Divine Advantage.

The Shunammite woman was spared the agony of experiencing a seven-year famine in the land of Israel because of favour.

Prophet Elisha, the man of God, whose ministry she supported, favoured her and gave her first-hand grapevine information about the famine coming into the land. He further advised her to leave with her household and go and sojourn anywhere she wanted until the famine was over.

As a result, she went to dwell in the land of the Philistines until the famine was over (See 2 Kings 8:1-3). She never suffered any famine or setback during or after the famine because favour gave her divine advantage.

Similarly, the children of Reuben and the children of Gad received their inheritance on the East side of the Jordan before their other brethren through a stroke of favour.

When they saw the land of Jazer and the land of Gilead, that indeed the region *was* a place for livestock, they approached Moses, Eliezer, the priest, and the leaders of the congregation with their request, saying,

"If we have found favor in your sight, let this land be given to your servants as a possession. Do not take us over the Jordan" (Numbers 32:1-5).

So "Moses gave to the children of Gad, to the children of Reuben, and to half the tribe of Manasseh the son of Joseph, the kingdom of Sihon king of the Amorites and the kingdom of Og king of Bashan, the land with its cities within the borders, the cities of the surrounding country" (Numbers 32:33).

15. Favour Distinguishes People From The Crowd. It was God's favour on the New Testament Church that distinguished them from others in their time.

We read, "So continuing daily with one accord in the temple, and breaking bread from house to house, they ate their food with gladness and simplicity of heart, praising God and having favor with all the people. And the Lord added to the church daily those who were being saved" (Acts 2:46-47);

"For if by the one man's offense death reigned through the one, much more those who receive abundance of grace and of the gift of righteousness will reign in life through the One, Jesus Christ" (Romans 5:17).

16. Favour Brings Royal Approval. Because of favour, **Joseph** received approval from Pharaoh to travel from Egypt to Canaan with his brothers and many others to bury his father, Jacob (Genesis 50:4-8). He also gave his father a most befitting burial (Genesis 50:9-11).

Through prayer and fasting, **Nehemiah** received favour from God. And through favour that resulted from his prayer to God specifically concerning his approaching the king, he received the king's approval, including diplomatic permits, financial and material resources, to travel home to Judah to repair the broken down walls of Jerusalem (See Nehemiah 1:4-11; 2:4-8).

17. Favour Has Widespread Impact. Favour is so powerful that it affects the lives of not just the direct recipient, but also touches many other lives too. Sometimes people experience favour by coming in contact or associating with someone who is walking in favour.

Many examples abound in scripture to validate this point. Laban, Jacob's uncle, enjoyed favour with God which caused his livestock and household to increase because of his association with Jacob (Genesis 30:27-28).

Potiphar enjoyed blessings in his household because of his association with Joseph. We read, "So it was, from the time *that* he had made him overseer of his house and all that he had, that the LORD blessed the Egyptian's house for Joseph's sake; and the blessing of the LORD was on all that he had in the house and in the field. (Genesis 39:5).

18. Favour Brings Total Recovery. Favour is a mighty weapon of total recovery. David fully recovered all that the Amalekites looted from him and his men in their temporary homeland, Ziklag, when God's favour came upon him.

After his prayer, he received a prophetic word: "Pursue, for you shall surely overtake *them* and without fail recover *all*" (1 Samuel 30:8). Aware that God surrounds the righteous with the shield of favour (Psalm 5:12), David, along with some of his men, went with that covering of favour in pursuit of their enemies.

THE FAVOUR DIMENSION

On the way, they had another major favour encounter with a young man, an Egyptian, a servant of an Amalekite, abandoned by his master because he was ill. David's men ministered favour to this man by giving him bread to eat and water to drink.

In return, David received valuable help and escort from this man to the hideout of their enemies, where they mercilessly attacked and destroyed them and also recovered all that was stolen from them.

Scripture affirms, "So David recovered all that the Amalekites had carried away, and David rescued his two wives. And nothing of theirs was lacking, either small or great, sons or daughters, spoil or anything which they had taken from them; David recovered all" (1 Samuel 30:18-19).

19. Favour Brings Healing. King Hezekiah received a bad report from the Lord through the prophet Elijah that he was going to die from his sickness (2 Kings 20:1). But he prayed and wept bitterly before the Lord, asking Him to heal him. God favoured him and answered his prayer—healed him and added fifteen more years to his life. He also promised to protect and defend him and his nation from their enemies (See 2 Kings 20:2-7).

20. Favour Cancels Out Negative Reports. When you receive a negative doctor's report, parking contravention charge, debt collection threats, or legal sentences, etc. only favour from God can wipe out these facts and their effect on your life.

That was the case in King Hezekiah's example

cited before. Favour cancelled out the bad report he got from Elijah. When favour shows up through God's anointing, healing flows to negate the doctor's report, parking charges are reversed, legal charges dropped or drastically reduced, and debts cancelled.

Here is a glorious report: "Praise God! Thank you, Rev'd. Ifeoma, for your faith, your prayers, and your prophecies. I attended your R.O.R.M.I. Southport Healing Glory Outpouring Rally on Saturday 20th May 2017 to give thanks and praise to God for what He did for me following your prayers for me.

The Lord upheld me in court where I was alone, no support, no solicitor, and all the odds were against me. There, He poured out His mercy and granted me favour and blessings from the judge, as you prayed would happen"—S.K., Dukinfield.

21. Favour Brings Resurrection From The Dead.
Dorcas was raised from the dead through God's favour when Peter prayed for her. A very unique slant to Dorcas' story is that she was a very generous woman who invested her resources into the house of God and ministered favour to other peoples' lives.

So when death struck, at a time Dorcas could not fight for herself, those she ministered to rose up to fight on her behalf. The church would not allow the devil to rob them of a sister so addicted to ministering favour to others.

They simply refused the report of her death and rather sent for Peter to come and pray for her to be raised up from the dead. In fact, when Peter arrived at the scene, the women were weeping and showed him all the things Dorcas made for the church i.e. evidences of her seeds of favour.

So when Peter prayed, resurrection favour came upon Dorcas and she was raised up from the dead and presented to the church alive to the glory of God (See Acts 9: 36-41).

Also, favour came upon the widow of Nain. Consequently, her dead son was raised from the dead by Jesus. In fact the Bible declares, "When the Lord saw her, He had compassion on her and said to her, "Do not weep." Then He came and touched the open coffin, and those who carried *him* stood still.

And He said, "Young man, I say to you, arise." So he who was dead sat up and began to speak. And He presented him to his mother" (Luke 7:13-15). Favour brought about the resurrection of Lazarus from the dead by Jesus (John 11:38-44). Scripture alluded to the fact that Jesus loved Lazarus (John 11:3, 35-36).

22. Favour Brings Freedom From Bondage. Any manner of bondage or addiction can be broken when favour shows up. The mad man of Gadare was healed and delivered from bondage to over two thousand demons when Jesus encountered him, releasing the favour of God upon him (See Mark 5: 1-20).

When he requested to follow Jesus after he received his healing, Jesus told him to "Go home to your friends, and tell them what great things the Lord has done for you, and how He has had compassion on you. "And he departed and began to proclaim in Decapolis all that Jesus had done for him; and all marvelled" (Mark 5:18-20).

Sure, the people marvelled at the immensity of God's favour and love that healed and set that man free and made him a delight to be with. Today, drug addicts and people bound up by the enemy in any way are still set free through the flow of God's favour onto them.

Among other examples, I know of an ex-alcoholic who was set free from bondage to that demon of alcoholism through prayers. God's favour came upon her, healed and set her free completely. Now, He is using her to minister His favour to others, bringing them needed healing and encouragement. Hallelujah!

23. Favour Replenishes Empty Storehouse. Have you ever experienced empty store house or bank account? Have you experienced those moments when at your time of need, someone takes you out for shopping or does it for you at their own expense?

Have you experienced unexpected raise or promotion in your place of work? Have you experienced a business sales boom? All these are finger-prints of favour worth cherishing and giving God thanks for, if you have, or when you experience any of them.

24. Favour Empowers One To Make Wise Choices And Ultimately Get The Best Results. To show how much God honuors the marriage institution on the earth, He attached favour to undergird the man who makes the right decision to get a wife:

"He who finds a true and faithful] wife finds a good thing And obtains favor *and* approval from the LORD"

THE FAVOUR DIMENSION

(Proverbs 18:22, AMP).

25. Favour Delivers One From Divine Judgement.
Noah was spared from being destroyed along with the people of his day because of God's favour:

"Then the LORD saw that the wickedness of man *was* great in the earth, and *that* every intent of the thoughts of his heart *was* only evil continually. And the LORD was sorry that He had made man on the earth, and He was grieved in His heart.

So the LORD said, "I will destroy man whom I have created from the face of the earth, both man and beast, creeping thing and birds of the air, for I am sorry that I have made them." But Noah found grace in the eyes of the LORD" (Genesis 6:5-8, see also vs. 13-21).

In another context, we read, "Then certain of the elders of the land rose up and spoke to all the assembly of the people, saying: "Micah of Moresheth prophesied in the days of Hezekiah king of Judah, and spoke to all the people of Judah, saying, 'Thus says the LORD of hosts: "Zion shall be plowed *like* a field, Jerusalem shall become heaps of ruins, And the mountain of the temple Like the bare hills of the forest.""

Did Hezekiah king of Judah and all Judah ever put him to death? Did he not fear the LORD and seek the LORD's favor? And the LORD relented concerning the doom which He had pronounced against them" (Jeremiah 26:17-19).

26. Favour Brings Peace And Joy To Our Lives.
Favour always produces comfort, wholeness, re-

assurance, peace, and joy like nothing else can.

Often, we take the peace of God on our lives for granted. But we need to discern that this is a result of God's favour: "You will keep *him* in perfect peace, *Whose* mind *is* stayed *on You,* Because he trusts in You ... Therefore, having been justified by faith, we have peace with God through our Lord Jesus Christ" (Isaiah 26:3; Romans 5:1).

Joy is a spontaneous outburst of pleasure or satisfaction when we hear any news or receive any gift of value to us. Joy is a fruit of the Holy Spirit given to empower us in our daily lives. Remarkably, the early disciples, regardless of the persecution they experienced, "were filled with joy and with the Holy Spirit" (Acts 13:52).

Joy is a product of God's love and favour. Thus we need to always give God thanks for any moment of His peace and joy we enjoy in our lives, families, homes, and environments

27. Favour Brings Supernatural Harvest. After the death of Jesus, his disciples, led by Peter, went back to their fishing business. That night on the sea, they caught nothing (John 21: 3). It must have been frustrating for them.

But when Jesus showed up the next morning, favour stepped in with Him to change their story for good. Following His instruction to cast their net on the right side of their boat, they cast their net, "and now they were not able to draw it in because of the multitude of fish" (John 21:6).

In addition, on coming back to shore "they saw a fire of coals there, and fish laid on it, and bread" (John 21:9).

That is having cooked breakfast without labour. They also enjoyed the privilege of being invited by Jesus to share that breakfast with Him—all because of favour. Do you need supernatural harvest in any area of your life? Then begin to expect God's favour to rain upon you in that area, call it in and receive it in Jesus name!

28. Favour Delivers One From Lowly Place Into The Palace. Favour is such a strong force that it can literally deliver you from a lowly place, a place of deprivation, degradation, worthlessness, isolation, lack, brokenness, and despair, and lift you into the palace.

And the cool thing about it is that it does so without recourse to any negative report about you or contradiction in your life. Such was the experience of Mephibosheth, Jonathan's son. Favour located him while he was still in Lo Debar and launched him into the palace.

In spite of the negative report about him from Ziba, who would not mention his name to David, but only referred to him as one lame in his feet, and dwelling at Lo Debar (2 Samuel 9:3-4), King David sent for Mephibosheth and permanently relocated him from Lo Debar to the palace, where he also enjoyed all the other royal privileges exclusive to the king's sons (2 Samuel 9:5-13). Glory to God!

Thus, people may not mention your name when occasion demands it to someone in a position to bless you, but favour steps in to locate you into your covenant wealthy place for good.

Always remember that your physical weakness is not a limitation to God. Your disadvantage is God's advantage.

29. Favour Safeguards One From Premature Death: The prophet Jeremiah, on many occasions, faced vicious attacks from his countrymen who were opposed to his ministry. The attacks were all designed to kill him prematurely. But through favour released upon him by God, his life was spared over and over again.

For example, during the reign of King Jehoiakim of Judah, the priests, false prophets, and nobles of the land were so offended by his prophetic message and rose up against him.

We read, " … when Jeremiah had made an end of speaking all that the LORD had commanded *him* to speak to all the people, that the priests and the prophets and all the people seized him, saying, "You will surely die! Why have you prophesied in the name of the LORD, saying, 'This house shall be like Shiloh, and this city shall be desolate, without an inhabitant'?" And all the people were gathered against Jeremiah in the house of the LORD.

When the princes of Judah heard these things, they came up from the king's house to the house of the LORD and sat down in the entry of the New Gate of the LORD's *house.* And the priests and the prophets spoke to the princes and all the people, saying, "This man deserves to die! For he has prophesied against this city, as you have heard with your ears" (Jeremiah 26:8-11).

Thankfully, favour stepped in and turned the hearts of the princes and the people to speak against the plans of the priests and prophets, and subsequently spared Jeremiah's life, using Ahikam, the son of Shaphan.

Thus we read, "Nevertheless the hand of Ahikam the son of Shaphan was with Jeremiah, so that they should not give him into the hand of the people to put him to death" (Jeremiah 6:24).

30. Favour Makes Impossibilities Become Possible. God's favour makes things happen for us that would have been impossible. Think about **Abraham and Sarah,** having their promised child, Isaac at a time when naturally speaking it was impossible:

"Therefore *it is* of faith that *it might be* according to grace, so that the promise might be sure to all the seed, not only to those who are of the law, but also to those who are of the faith of Abraham, who is the father of us all (as it is written,

"I have made you a father of many nations") in the presence of Him whom he believed—God, who gives life to the dead and calls those things which do not exist as though they did; who, contrary to hope, in hope believed, so that he became the father of many nations, according to what was spoken, "So shall your descendants be" (Romans 4:16-18).

Our Lord Jesus Christ was a product of God's favour

coming upon His mother, Mary, a virgin: "Then the angel said to her, "Do not be afraid, Mary, for you have found favor with God. And behold, you will conceive in your womb and bring forth a Son, and shall call His name Jesus" (Luke 1:30-31).

31. Favour Brings Satisfaction In Life. In the words of the blessing Moses pronounced on the tribe of Naphtali, we read, " ... of Naphtali he said: "O Naphtali, satisfied with favor, And full of the blessing of the LORD, Possess the west and the south" (Deuteronomy 33:23).

32. Favour Empowers Us To Accomplish Our Dreams. True vision from God is never accomplished independently of Him. Because His visions or plans for us are always loftier than our natural abilities, we will always need His favour to accomplish them.

Thus, I want to testify to the glory of God, that through His supply of favour I am alive and saved today, and serving Him on earth.

Through His favour, He enabled me to write and publish **29 books,** hundreds of newsletters, many magazine articles, tracts, Facebook and LinkedIn posts, blog posts, poems, etc., all of which have many testimonies received from people who have been, and are still being impacted by them globally.

Through His favour, I received from the Holy Spirit over a thousand six hundred and thirty **(1,630),** authentic **Songs of Glory,** which I have documented. By His grace, I have recorded and produced **15 amazing Songs of Glory music CDs,** and one musical video as at the time of writing this book.

Although I have shared this testimony in a previous book, I feel it is necessary to share it here again as it is specifically related to favour. This was the miracle of favour that birthed one of my songs, **Favour Is My Name,** the title track of one of my Albums, also contained in my Songbook and devotional Guide, **Songs Of Glory Vol. One: 1,012 Heavenly Downloads Of The Holy Spirit From The Throne Of Grace**.

On Wednesday, 11th November 2015 at 10.29 a.m., my husband had travelled to a town to meet the bookbinders regarding my book, **Honey From The Wilderness,** to get them to bind up the books he took to them.

While there, the man who was to do it, and who had told me to ask my husband to come with the books, told him he could not do it that day. That meant he was to return to Manchester and go back another day for that job, a situation which could have frustrated our plan to get the books finished on time and have adequate time to prepare for our impending Conference.

When he called me on the phone and informed me of what the man said, I immediately rejected it and went straight into prayer and spiritual warfare, binding the enemy and reversing his plot in Jesus name.

I prayed for God's favour to move in the situation and get the man to agree to do the job for us. To the glory of God, a few minutes after I finished praying, my husband called me back and told me that the man had decided to do the work for us and had asked him to come back for it in two hours' time. "Praise God, I screamed on the phone."

We both rejoiced, knowing it was an answer to prayer. He just decided to drive around somewhere in the town while the job was being done. He later on went back and got the books, all perfectly bound the same day. As soon as I came off the phone speaking with my husband, this song, *Favour Is My Name,* exploded from my spirit out of my mouth.

So I joyfully sang it over and over again and right there recorded it to my phone, and also played it for my husband on his return, and he enjoyed it. This song carries an awesome anointing of favour on it.

It had such a profound impact on me, and I began to share with it others who also enjoyed it, being greatly blessed by it. Later on, I decided to record it in my **Songs Of Glory 6 CD Album, Favour Is My Name.**

While in Nigeria in February 2016, accompanied by my earthly mum, one of my sisters and her husband, among others, we recorded the musical video of this original song. Many people's lives have been greatly transformed through this song, which is now being used in different churches, meetings, etc. To God be the glory!

Although I have mentioned the genesis of my Songs of Glory in some of my previous books, I need to reiterate here that it was mainly through God's favour I received them, and was also able to accomplish a long-awaited dream of over 20 years, which was to publish a unique, anointed prophetic Songbook and Devotional guide that contains many of these songs which cover a wide variety of subject-matter, given to me by the Holy Spirit.

Consequently, **Songs Of Glory Vol. One: 1,012 Heavenly Downloads Of The Holy Spirit From The Throne Of Grace,** was successfully launched during our R.O.R.M.I. Healing Glory Conference on Saturday, 17th December 2016.

This Songbook and Devotional Guide is now being used for worship in our Ministry meetings and events, impacting lives in our events and all around the globe through the songs contained in it.

And here is a testimony about the book: "Praise to God for the wonderful and precious Songbook and Devotional Guide by Apostle Ifeoma Fiiriter, **Songs of Glory Vol. One: 1,012 Heavenly Downloads of the Holy Spirit From The Throne of Grace:**

"When Apostle Ifeoma gave me this book, on my way back home, as I opened this book to read it on the train, I felt the anointing of God shooting through my fingers. Since then, the Lord has taken me on an incredible spiritual journey.

The songs in the book are incredibly powerful and just minister to you as you read or sing them. I use the book in the morning, and I just get lost in the presence of God, worshiping, singing, and praying in tongues.

I am so grateful to have such a powerful resource available for me to use. Each time, there is an excitement and anticipation in my spirit I cannot comprehend, and I look forward to worshiping God, using this Songbook.

Thank you, Apostle Ifeoma, for this powerful Songbook and devotional guide. May God bless you exceedingly and give you continual increase and uncommon favour in your Ministry in Jesus Mighty Name, Amen"—G.E., Liverpool.

Let me add that this 380-page anointed, prophetic Songbook & Devotional Guide covers a tremendous variety of subject-matter, and is suitable for worship/ music ministers, individuals, families, leaders, churches, ministries, schools at all levels, businesses, etc.

I can truly say that God favoured me even in the content of these songs. They are so exceptionally unique, sweet, anointed, glorious, clear in their divine messages, powerful, and highly relevant to mans' needs.

These songs carry the DNA of Almighty God, and are God's direct life-line to people in dire situations. Many of the songs are clear prophetic messages from the Father to His people. Some depict revival and glory outpouring cultures.

Some are songs of consecration, devotion, salvation, healing, deliverance, spiritual warfare and breakthroughs. Some are psalms, victory strategies, revelations about the Holy Spirit, Jesus Christ's birth, the power of His name, blood, resurrection, His second coming, the integrity of the Word of God, etc.

These songs, whether sung or read, carry unusual grace about them that make them life-transformers to people. Just by reading, meditating and embracing the words of these songs peoples' lives are greatly impacted.

The genesis and evolution of these songs, the unique contexts in which many of these songs were received, amazing testimonies from some of these songs, and other very powerful nuggets of wisdom on how to function as God's true and effective worshiper, are included in this resource and also in my book, **"Power Of Extravagant Praise And Worship: A Taste Of Songs Of Glory"** (2nd Edition),.

These invaluable timeless resources including our **Songs Of Glory CDs** can be ordered by phone, post, or from http://www.favourbooksandmusic.com or FavourLandBooks on Amazon.

Let me add that **God, through His favour, trained me to be play the keyboard.** He has, over the years, enabled me to both sing and play the keyboard while recording the CD Albums of some of these awesome **Songs of Glory** He gave to me.

Through favour, God has empowered me to minister effectively, leading in worship, using the keyboard, singing and playing many of these amazing songs at our Ministry events, services, at some other Ministry's events, and also during my weekly Facebook Live Broadcasts, reaching and impacting countless lives globally to His glory.

33. Favour Turns One's Mess Into A Glorious Message. Any unpleasant situation or mess can be turned around through God's favour. Here is a powerful testimony to attest to this truth:

"I am writing to give thanks to God for what He did for me through the Robe of Righteousness Ministries Int'l. I was studying Nursing for two years at a certain University. I did not complete my training because I did not pass all of the modules.

Thereafter, I received letters that I had been over-paid in training, and I was required to pay back two thousand seven hundred pounds (£2,700). I contacted Rev Ifeoma and informed her of my bleak situation. She prayed with me for God's divine intervention in the matter.

She subsequently advised me to write to those who were funding my training and explain to them why I did not owe them that money and request them to waive off the debt. I wrote to them as advised, but they kept writing back to me telling me that they would not accept to cancel the debt of £2,700.

When I informed Rev Ifeoma about their further decision, she asked me to go to the Students Union office and ask for advice regarding the matter. By this time, I was fed up because it seemed as if nothing was working.

But Rev. Ifeoma assured me that God would fight for me in this matter and give me victory. Reluctantly, I went to the Students Union Office, and on my second visit, I was able to speak to one of the advisors who agreed to launch a complaint through the University for me, saying that this was not guaranteed to give me the results I needed, and that it could also take a long time.

Nevertheless, I launched the complaint, and my advisor was able to write to those who were funding my training to ask them to stop writing to me until the investigation was over. After this, Revs. Ifeoma & Pastor Daniel felt led to do a debt-burning service during the Ministry's twenty-one day fast in January 2008.

I was asked to bring evidence of any debt I had. So I took one of the letters which I had received from those who were funding my training requesting for £2,700 repayment to that Tabernacle of Glory Service in Chester on Sunday, the 20th of January.

There, Rev Ifeoma & Pastor Daniel prayed for debt cancellation miracles for me and for others who had the same need. All our letters representing our debts were burnt in the presence of the Lord. I went home hopeful that God would grant me the victory.

Before the end of March 2008, when I had almost forgotten, the University wrote to me saying that they accepted that they were at fault, and that they would write to those who were funding my training to inform them that they accepted responsibility for the over-payment.

Thus, the £2,700 debt was supernaturally cancelled for me by Almighty God. As I write this testimony, all I feel like doing is shouting and shouting and praising God for the marvelous miracle that He did for me through the Robe of Righteousness Ministries Int'l. My heart is so full of joy and I give God all the glory.

I thank Rev. Ifeoma and God for not giving up on me, even though I was losing faith at times. I encourage people to partner with this life changing Ministry." — M. C., Liverpool.

To God be all the glory for this marvellous testimony of God's favour released upon this dear sister. Let me also share this testimony of favour received by one of our Ministry partners some years ago. Then, her husband was in Africa, and needed a visa to come over and join her in the U.K.

However, all circumstances were terribly against her. For over three years she had been struggling to get her husband back into the country to no avail.

In fact, it did look completely humanly impossible, as the UK Home Office and the British High Commission in Ghana refused to consent to an appeal to allow him to come back into the country. In addition to this, our dear partner's bank account was in the red, overdrawn.

Nevertheless, the Lord led me to prophesy favour over her in one of our meetings in Manchester and also in Chester at the time, telling her that her husband would receive his visa to come over to the UK, and that God would also bless her financially.

Sequel to this, the door of favour swung open before her. Someone in her office whom she never considered a friend blessed her with some money, and several others gave her money to her utter amazement. More than that, even the British High Commission's insistence for her to send her bank account details, which she failed to respond to, did not stop God from getting them to approve the visa.

On the day of this miracle, God supernaturally used somebody else hand-picked by Him to issue the visa to him. To cap it all up, God led me again to prophesy that she would not borrow the money for His ticket, but that it would come as a result of God's favour.

To the glory of God, this word was fulfilled by the God of divine favour whom we serve.

CHAPTER 6

EXCEEDING ABUNDANT GRACE OF GOD

I know this book is specifically on the Favour Dimension. However, because favour is an aspect of grace, both being very closely related, I feel led to include here some powerful insights the Lord gave me some time ago about **grace** i.e. the exceeding power and benefits of His grace.

This is so you can fully understand the subject of the favour of God and its broader extension—grace, so you can maximize both effectively to God's glory. **Let me reiterate that** grace is more than favour. Grace is always a free gift of God while favour can be earned sometimes.

And now, to the revelation the Lord gave me about the benefits of His exceeding abundant grace.

From the Bible, we discover a number of things about **grace:**

1. Grace is your exit from scheduled judgement. We read, "Then the LORD saw that the wickedness of man *was* great in the earth, and *that* every intent of the thoughts of his heart *was* only evil continually. And the LORD was sorry that He had made man on the earth, and He was grieved in His heart.

So the LORD said, "I will destroy man whom I have

created from the face of the earth, both man and beast, creeping thing and birds of the air, for I am sorry that I have made them." But Noah found grace in the eyes of the LORD" (Genesis 6:5-8).

By grace, God spared Lot and his family during the destruction of Sodom and Gomorrah because He remembered Abraham: "And it came to pass, when God destroyed the cities of the plain, that God remembered Abraham, and sent Lot out of the midst of the overthrow, when He overthrew the cities in which Lot had dwelt" (Genesis 19:29).

2. Grace is your access to divine secrets. Genesis 6:13-23 tells us: " ... God said to Noah, "The end of all flesh has come before Me, for the earth is filled with violence through them; and behold, I will destroy them with the earth.

Make yourself an ark of gopherwood; make rooms in the ark, and cover it inside and outside with pitch. And this is how you shall make it: The length of the ark *shall be* three hundred cubits, its width fifty cubits, and its height thirty cubits.

You shall make a window for the ark, and you shall finish it to a cubit from above; and set the door of the ark in its side. You shall make it *with* lower, second, and third *decks.* And behold, I Myself am bringing floodwaters on the earth, to destroy from under heaven all flesh in which *is* the breath of life; everything that *is* on the earth shall die.

But I will establish My covenant with you; and you shall go into the ark—you, your sons, your wife, and your sons' wives with you. And of every living thing of all flesh you shall bring two of every *sort* into the ark, to keep *them* alive with you; they shall be male and female ... And you shall take for yourself of all food that is eaten, and you shall gather *it* to yourself; and it shall be food for you and for them." Thus Noah did; according to all that God commanded him, so he did"

Noah was spared from judgement because of the grace of God upon him which gave him access to His divine secrets.

3. Grace is your access to God's greatest gift of salvation: "But God, who is rich in mercy, because of His great love with which He loved us, even when we were dead in trespasses, made us alive together with Christ (by grace you have been saved) ... For by grace you have been saved through faith, and that not of yourselves; *it is* the gift of God, not of works, lest anyone should boast" (Ephesians 2:4-5, 8-9).

4. Grace is your exit from the curse: "Christ has redeemed us from the curse of the law, having become a curse for us (for it is written, "Cursed *is* everyone who hangs on a tree"), that the blessing of Abraham might come upon the Gentiles in Christ Jesus, that we might receive the promise of the Spirit through faith" (Galatians 3:13-14).

5. Grace is your exit from poverty: "For you know the grace of our Lord Jesus Christ, that though He was rich, yet for your sakes He became poor, that you through His poverty might become rich" (2 Corinthians 8:9).

6. Grace is your guaranteed access to divine healing and health: "who Himself bore our sins in His own body on the tree, that we, having died to sins, might live for righteousness—by whose stripes you were healed" (1 Peter 2:24).

7. Grace empowers you to reign in life: "For if by the one man's offense death reigned through the one, much more those who receive abundance of grace and of the gift of righteousness will reign in life through the One, Jesus Christ.)" (Romans 5:17).

8. Grace is your entry ticket to a lifestyle of heaven on earth: "Grace and peace be multiplied to you in the knowledge of God and of Jesus our Lord, as His divine power has given to us all things that *pertain* to life and godliness, through the knowledge of Him who called us by glory and virtue, by which have been given to us exceedingly great and precious promises, that through these you may be partakers of the divine nature

... The LORD will give grace and glory; No good *thing* will He withhold From those who walk uprightly" (2 Peter 1:2-4; Psalms 84:11).

9. Grace is your ticket to effective service in God's kingdom. Scripture reveals that Jesus "grew and became strong in spirit, filled with wisdom; and the grace of God was upon Him" (Luke 2:40).

Paul declared, " ... I am the least of the apostles, who am not worthy to be called an apostle, because I persecuted the church of God. But by the grace of God I am what I am, and His grace toward me was not in vain; but I labored more abundantly than they all, yet not I, but the grace of God *which was* with me. .. And God *is* able to make all grace abound toward you, that you, always having all sufficiency in all *things,* may have an abundance for every good work" (1 Corinthians 15:9-10; 2 Corinthians 9:8).

10. Grace is your proven weapon of warfare to pull down every satanic mountain or stronghold blocking your destiny: "This *is* the word of the LORD to Zerubbabel: 'Not by might nor by power, but by My Spirit,' Says the LORD of hosts. 'Who *are* you, O great mountain? Before Zerubbabel *you shall become* a plain! And he shall bring forth the capstone With shouts of "Grace, grace to it!"'" (Zechariah 4:6-7).

11. Grace is your access to a lifetime of enjoying limitless assets and doing great exploits: "And God *is* able to make all grace abound toward you, that you, always having all sufficiency in all *things,* may have an abundance for every good work" (2 Corinthians 9:8).

12. Grace is God's intentional bias to favour you in spite of who you are or what you have done. Thus God enabled Abraham and Sarah to bear Isaac even when they had passed the age of child bearing:

" ... Sarah herself also received strength to conceive seed, and she bore a child when she was past the age, because she judged Him faithful who had promised. Therefore from one man, and him as good as dead, were born *as many* as the stars of the sky in multitude— innumerable as the sand which is by the seashore" (Hebrews 11:11-12).

13. Grace enables you to overcome sin and live holy. It is not a license for sin as some people think, but rather a divine empowerment to live holy on earth:

" ... Noah found grace in the eyes of the LORD. This is the genealogy of Noah. Noah was a just man, perfect in his generations. Noah walked with God ... Then the LORD said to Noah, "Come into the ark, you and all your household, because I have seen *that* you *are* righteous before Me in this generation" (Genesis 6:8-9; 7:1).

God imparted grace to King Abimelech which restrained him from having intimate relationship with Sarah, although Abraham and Sarah played into his hands: "And God said to him in a dream, "Yes, I know that you did this in the integrity of your heart. For I also withheld you from sinning against Me; therefore I did not let you touch her" (Genesis 20:6).

14. Grace is a product of the holy and sacrificial work of Jesus Christ to restore you to God's original plan to be a part of His family on earth. It is a product of God's covenant sacrifice of the shed blood of Jesus:

"being justified freely by His grace through the redemption that is in Christ Jesus, whom God set forth *as* a propitiation by His blood, through faith, to demonstrate His righteousness, because in His forbearance God had passed over the sins that were previously committed, to demonstrate at the present time His righteousness, that He might be just and the justifier of the one who has faith in Jesus" (Romans

3:24-26).

15. Because of grace, God remembers you in your affliction or trouble, and plans a way of escape or victory for you: "Then God remembered Noah, and every living thing, and all the animals that *were* with him in the ark. And God made a wind to pass over the earth, and the waters subsided.

The fountains of the deep and the windows of heaven were also stopped, and the rain from heaven was restrained. And the waters receded continually from the earth. At the end of the hundred and fifty days the waters decreased ... Then God spoke to Noah, saying, "Go out of the ark, you and your wife, and your sons and your sons' wives with you" (Genesis 8:1-3, 15).

16. Grace enables you to multiply and walk in dominion: "So God blessed Noah and his sons, and said to them: "Be fruitful and multiply, and fill the earth. And the fear of you and the dread of you shall be on every beast of the earth, on every bird of the air, on all that move *on* the earth, and on all the fish of the sea. They are given into your hand.

Every moving thing that lives shall be food for you. I have given you all things, even as the green herbs" (Genesis 9:1-3). Amazing what God's **grace** can do in and through our lives!

THE FAVOUR DIMENSION

CHAPTER 7

STREAMS OF FAVOUR ON REAL LIVES THROUGH R.O.R.M.I.

I mentioned in chapter 5 a few testimonies of people who received favour through our Ministry, Robe Of Righteousness Ministries Int'l.

Here, I want to share more testimonies of people who have been overtaken by God's streams of favour flowing through our Ministry. I believe that you will be encouraged and blessed reading them, and ultimately expect and receive your breakthrough favour too.

"Dear Rev Ifeoma, I had wonderful favour on 25th January 2015. We had prayed together about the badly blocked drains. I reported a blockage because I had seen a help number on the matter. When they arrived, I asked for whatever help they could give with it. In return, I had it unblocked and cleansed for free. I thank God for His direction, provision, and intervention!"— J.H., Southport.

"Dear Rev. Ifeoma, I want to thank God for what He did for me. During the past six weeks I had to spend a large part of my wages to help two special children in need. I was promised by the organisation I took care of the children for that I would be reimbursed, but it was not forth-coming. I thought I had said goodbye to the cash, bearing in mind that there is only one wage in my home. I did not begrudge this at all as I love the children.

Rev. Ifeoma, you prayed, declaring that I would be reimbursed every penny I spent. Two days after, every penny was returned into my bank account. I stand in awe of God's mercy and kindness: "For He will deliver the needy when he cries, The poor also, and him who has no helper" (Psalm 72:12)—S.K., Dukinfield.

"*P*raise the Lord! I would like to thank God for His goodness towards me, using His anointed servant, Apostle Ifeoma Fiiriter. Truly, the love of God is amazing and His mercies endure forever. Since I became a part of the Robe of Righteousness Ministries Int'l, it has been my desire to move to Manchester and serve God fully there. I had been applying for jobs with no success.

When I eventually got called for an interview for a certain post, I decided not to take the job because it required me to work on weekends, which I did not want. I wanted my weekends to be free so that I will be able to go to church, and also be available to serve God in other ways.

I kept on applying until I finally got a job which seemed to fit my requirements (so I thought). Indeed, when I started, I didn't work weekends which was perfect.

Later on, I discovered that they wanted me to work on weekends. The moment I told my manager that I could not work during the weekends, the enemy attacked my relationship with her.

The rota was changed that week and I was put to work every weekend. Every attempt to get a weekend off seemed to fall on deaf ears. I spoke to Apostle Ifeoma and informed her of the challenges I was facing.

Because I could not get any weekends off, I could not be part of the music worship project which was taking place in the Ministry at the time. I felt down and depressed.

I was in tears and I went home tired and exhausted, thinking, "Lord I really missed being a part of this exciting project." On top of all this, I was facing financial challenges. Therefore, I didn't have money to go to work. The next day, Sunday, I felt worse and was not able to go to work. The devil told me it was all over with my job.

In fact, he tried to replay in my head the last conversation I had with my manager, when she told me that if I was absent from work for any reason, no matter what it was, I would get a verbal warning and possibly be dismissed from work.

That evening, as I was still depressed, I received a call from Apostle Ifeoma. At this time, I was already thinking negatively in my mind and speaking with my mouth that it was all over. On hearing me, Apostle Ifeoma, declared, "you will not be sacked, those that want you to leave, they themselves will leave before you. You will leave in honour and not dishonour." She encouraged me to repent before God about the way I was speaking before, which I did. She also advised me to contact the manager on Monday, which I did.

Soon after my dialogue with the Lord's servant, Apostle Ifeoma, I managed to get hold of my manager. To my utter amazement, right there over the phone, she changed the rota to favour me. For the day I was not able to go to work, she gave me authorised leave to cover me.

I could not reconcile in my mind how it happened. The same manager who was telling me I could not be absent for any reason, God through His servant, turned her around to favour me. What the devil meant for evil God turned around for my good.

Apostle Ifeoma said "Marah can be turned to sweet water", and indeed it was, by the power of the anointed prophetic word that came through God's servant. Thank you, Apostle Ifeoma.

May the Lord continue to bless and use you mightily! I am certain that if it was not for God's intervention through your life, this could have been a sad story. To God be the glory!"—M.C., Liverpool

"*I* attended the Eminent Ladies Anointed Bible Study in Manchester and enjoyed the time with the Lord there. At the end of the meeting, Rev'd. Ifeoma gave me her book, **Baptism Of The Holy Spirit: Embracing The Power and Purpose of Speaking In Tongues.** After reading the book, I began to pray in tongues and I have been praying in tongues more and more since then. It's a great thing to walk in the Spirit and to move in the Spirit.

I had a problem with my solar panels and it was not my fault. The fault was with the people who fitted them in, and I had paid them money for it but they were not acknowledging it. They said I was going to have to pay again, which means I was going to lose a lot of money.

The miracle is, from reading the book, **Baptism Of The Holy Spirit: Embracing The Power and Purpose of Speaking In Tongues,** I was praying in tongues, and I didn't even know what I was praying about, but the Lord knew.

Well, they phoned me and said they were going to give me £1,500 pounds. Later on, they called me again and said they were going to give me £6,500. They raised it!

Another miracle is, I had lost my keys and I couldn't find them. But as I prayed in tongues, the Holy Spirit helped me to find my keys! It's an exciting time!

Many people that I know don't like to pray in tongues because they don't understand it, but God understands. Thank you, very much, God bless you Rev'd. Ifeoma"—D.W., Preston.

"Praise the Lord. I would like to thank you, Apostle Ifeoma, for your prayers for me and my daughter over the years. I am very grateful, and pray that God will reward you richly for your love and support.

I would like to thank God for what He has done for me in the past few months. My daughter's bed was broken down and she had to use two mattresses to try to make it comfortable for her to sleep.

I also did not have a bed to sleep on. The old one had broken down and I was sleeping on the sofa for two years. My finances were not that good and I could not afford to get all of these items. My credit rating was not good so I was not able to get these items on credit either. I could not tell anyone about this situation. But the Lord knew about it.

The Year 2017 was incredible. After coming to the **''Favour Dimension''** Conference 2017 in Manchester, U.K., God removed the sackcloth of shame and reproach in my life.

Apostle Ifeoma decreed favour upon every family that attended the conference. I sat at the back of the church. But as she prayed and declared favour upon us, I claimed and received it.

To God be the glory, the stream of favour was released and I have been swimming in it ever since. When I got back home a few weeks after the Conference, I got a letter from the housing association. It was the normal monthly newsletter which they send to their residents.

Sometimes I read it, and sometimes I don't. However, this time, as I read it, God opened my eyes to see a section which stated that an organisation could help people in need to get furniture. So I decided to use the information and contact the organisation.

When I contacted them, they took my information. I told them my daughter needed a bed and a wardrobe but I was ashamed to say I needed one as well. After the phone call, I was restless.

I felt the Lord prompting me to tell them everything I needed. So the next day I phoned them up and told them I needed a bed as well and a wardrobe. God gave me favour and they did not question me why I had not mentioned it before. The lady said she would do her best, but she would work on helping me to get a bed and bedroom furniture for my daughter first.

After a few weeks, a company had agreed to purchase a brand new bed for my daughter, and I was also getting cash deposited into my account to purchase bedroom furniture for her.

I was so full of joy and thankful for God's mighty hand of favour and divine intervention. My daughter was so happy when the bed arrived, and our God also provided someone to come and set up the bed for her free of charge.

Soon after, I went to the furniture shop to buy the bedroom furniture for her. On my arrival, they were having a big sale and wanted to get rid of some stock. I could not believe my eyes. The furniture was heavily discounted. My daughter got beautiful bedroom furniture for next to nothing.

A few weeks later the lady from the organisation that had helped me to apply for this furniture grant contacted me and said that she was now going to start applying for my own bed and bedroom furniture, and she would let me know the outcome. A month passed and I did not hear from her. I got impatient and a bit fed up.

The Lord blessed me with some money so I decided to go and buy myself a bed. The Lord showed me great mercy. I went to the same furniture shop where God helped me to get my daughter's furniture. I saw a beautiful King size décor bed. I said ''Lord thank You for helping me to get this bed.

I asked the manager for a discount on the bed. He immediately said no. I went outside of the shop and I prayed again and I said ''Lord despite what the manager has said, I believe You for favour.'' I went back into the shop and told one of the assistants that I was going to buy the bed.

The manager saw me and sent another worker to whisper in the ear of the assistant who was helping me ''Don't give her a discount, let her pay full price.'' I did not say anything. The lady scanned the barcode for the bed. To her amazement, the bed had been discounted online already on their system.

I was so full of joy. God gave me favour. I now have a beautiful bed to sleep on. I was so overwhelmed with joy when it got delivered. After sleeping for two years on a sofa, God changed my story. He gave me a beautiful bed to sleep on.

Every time I sleep on my bed, I am filled with gratitude. It all happened after the **"Favour Dimension"** Conference'. However, the Lord was not finished. I needed to replace the sofa as well. The one I had was not in good condition because of being overused.

The Lord directed me to a different furniture shop. I don't even know how I got there. All I know is that it was God's favour because I was not aware of this shop before. I walked in and told the man I needed some sofas.

He had some stock which he wanted to get rid of quickly to make room for new stock. At an incredible price, he offered me a new suite and said he will not charge me for delivery. I left the shop full of joy. God also ensured that I had enough finances to do everything I needed. In fact, God ensured that I did not lack in anyway. Thank You Jesus, my Lord.

After I had almost forgotten about the lady who said she was going to work on helping me to get a bed and bedroom furniture, I later got a call from her. She had found a company that had accepted to buy me a brand new double bed, bedroom furniture and bedding.

I said, "Father, You are awesome." Everything changed just like that. The bed arrived and is now in my spare room to be used if a guest comes because the Lord had given me already a bed to sleep on. She deposited money into my account to get the bedroom furniture and the bedding.

The Lord led me again to a furniture shop. I went there and there was a bedroom set of two large double wardrobes and a large dresser table with a huge mirror waiting for me. The entire set was discounted for me and I did not even ask for it.

The assistant who welcomed me in the shop said to

me, "if you want to get it, I will go and ask the manager if he can give you a discount." The bedroom furniture matches my bed.

I laughed and I said, "Father You thought of everything. The same with my daughter's, her bedroom furniture matches her bed." The Lord did it. He changed our lives. The day we came to the **''Favour Dimension''** Conference in Manchester in July 2017 everything changed for us, and I give Him the glory.

Thank you, Apostle Ifeoma, for hosting this Conference. Thank you for being a blessing to us. God has done so much for us through your Ministry, and I am very grateful. Once again, I pray for God to reward you greatly for all that you are doing in His Kingdom. Many thanks"— G. E. Liverpool.

"The last few months have been difficult financially and workwise. I know the Lord took me out of the last job. I used to work with criminals and everything. I have done that for eleven years, and I thought it was enough.

Then I went to do an administrative job in an office and I just felt it was not for me. I had enough and loved working with people. So I went to do care in the community for a while, and it wasn't for me as well. I loved working with the people there but did not like the politics of the job.

Then I went to do a similar job and it was similar. I said, "Lord, what is happening, where do You want me to go?"

I was praying the whole time. I knew I was also being refined in that fire as well. I was praying and saying, "when Lord, when?" My finances were really bad. I then went to do this agency job.

I thought I could do it. It was a job in a factory and I thought it was good and I could tell people about the Lord whilst I was there. I passed all the tests, including the Maths, and I don't even know how I did it.

I had to do a five day induction and five weeks training as well. During the induction, the trainer called me into another room with another lady. That was the Friday before the Eminent Ladies International Conference 2017 of 15th July, and said, "I don't think you are suitable for this job."

I felt so rejected and I said, "it's only been five days, can't you give me more time?" And I wasn't the slowest. It was very difficult. I had no leg to stand on, since it was an agency job.

So I just thanked them and began to cry my eyes out. They said "you are a lovely lady but this is not for you." I began to say, "Lord what is going to happen to me now. I have got my flat, a mortgage and bills to pay. How am I going to manage?"

I said, "Lord, okay, I trust You." But I also felt bad and threw myself on the floor, crying at home, feeling sorry for myself before the Lord.

On Saturday morning, I felt this heaviness. I also felt numb and rejected. I then felt the Holy Spirit say, "I want you to go to Apostle Ifeoma's Conference in Manchester."

THE FAVOUR DIMENSION

I said, "Holy Spirit, this is You. Ok, I will obey." I then began to move myself to get ready, and I said, "I am going." The theme of the Conference was **"The Favour Dimension."** As soon as I walked into the Conference venue I felt this peace, and I said, "yes Lord, You really want me to be here."

I was really blessed. Apostle Ifeoma prayed for me for favour for a job. So, on Monday after the Conference, I applied for this job at the Manchester Airport, Customer Services.

I thought I could do that, and it happened so fast. I was called for an interview at the Manchester Airport and they said, "we would like to take you." I just knew it was the Lord. His Favour at work! So I praise the Lord for His favour.

Also, at the Airport it was £8 a day for parking, which at the time I couldn't really afford. I went to get a parking ticket, but the machine would not let me pay. I went to the office the next day. Because I wanted to be honest and I didn't want them to be charged. I spoke to the lady at the office and the lady said I shouldn't worry. I was fine for that day as well. Praise God for His Favour!!"—S.K., Cheshire.

"*I* want to use this opportunity to appreciate the God of this Commission; Robe of Righteousness Ministries 'Int'l (R.O.R.M.I) for the way He brought me and my husband and our business outfit, Alpha and Omega Enterprise and Consult, Asaba, to limelight.

On the 10th of October, 2017, God gave me an

idea of going to showcase some of our agricultural products like processed corn flour, cassava flour, bean flour, plantain flour, Micro-livestock, e.g. snail, and equipment, e.g. tarpaulin fish tank, for the 2017 World Food Day Celebration/Exhibition.

Such an idea had never come to my mind since I joined the Delta State Civil Service Commission as a fisheries officer on June 5th, 2002. This is because I used to invite fishermen, fish-farmers, both micro- and macro-livestock farmers/processors, fabricators of fishing gears and equipment and food/cash crop producers and processors to attend.

Then, I decided to inform my husband and son who gave me the go-ahead to make an inquiry concerning the exhibition aspect of the programme on Friday 13th of October, 2017.

I went through the normal procedure of indicating my interest and I was given an invitation letter by the Assistant Chief Agricultural Officer (A.C.A.O) of the Local Government (Oshimili South L.G.A of Delta State of Nigeria).

On the 16th of October 2017, which was the World Food Day, we displayed a tarpaulin fish tank and snail (micro-livestock) through our business out-fit.

To God's glory, we took the first position in fabricators' exhibition with the tarpaulin fish tank with a cash gift of 12,000 naira, and second position with a cash gift of 8,000 naira for micro-livestock exhibition of snail.

I also went with some members of Nigeria

Association of Women Entrepreneurs (Delta State Chapter) being their present Secretary. God also gave us recognition and victory by making us take the 3rd position for the micro-livestock exhibition of snail with a cash gift of 5,000 naira.

I thank God for showing us great favour on this occasion. I thank God for our parents-in-the-Lord, Rev. Daniel and Apst. (Mrs.) Ifeoma Fiiriter, who are entrepreneurs, and have released the same unction to us through their constant prayers and advice for us to be enterprising and function very well in our area of calling. May God's name be praised and adored forever in our lives and endeavours in Jesus Christ's name, Amen"—T. E., Asaba, Nigeria.

"One day, I was suffering from a virus attack and I was really low in my spirit, no energy or strength. And I called on Pastor Ifeoma and asked if she could pray for me, and the very next morning, and even in the night time, I felt much better. It disappeared. It's gone. I give all the praises to God. Thank you for praying for me. God bless you"—C.M., Southport.

"Praise God for His marvellous and glorious works. I want to thank God for what He did for me and my family through Robe of Righteousness Ministries Int'l recently.

My Sister contacted me on Saturday the 28th of October 2017 and informed me she had found a lump in her breast. I told her not to worry and just begin to thank God for her healing. I also told her not to inform people, especially those that will speak negative things about the situation. She told me she had only told my Mum and not other people because she did not want them to give her wrong advice.

That day I was going to the **R.O.R.M.I. Healing Glory Outpouring Rally** in Southport. During the time for prayer at the Rally, I stepped forward on behalf of my Sister, and Apostle Ifeoma prayed for her, and declared that she would be healed and the lump be rooted out of her breast.

After the Rally, Apostle Ifeoma informed me to go and tell my Sister to check her body. For a while, I could not speak to my Sister because her mobile phone broke down. This concerned me. Apostle Ifeoma prayed for me to be able to get in touch with her again and she also said she believed that my Sister was well.

On boxing day, the 26th of December, I reconnected with my Sister on Facebook. She informed me that the lump disappeared the same week she had told me about it. I knew it was that moment in Southport I came forward for prayer and Apostle Ifeoma prayed for her it happened!

I am so overjoyed to be part of the Robe of Righteousness Ministries Int'l. This ministry is a life changer—a global solution centre. The day my sister told me about the lump was the day I was going to the Rally in Southport.

What if I had not been there at that meeting for some reason? It was at this God appointed and anointed Rally

God intervened for me in my Sister's case, to bring an answer—a supernatural solution to the problem.

Glory be to God! Thank you Jesus. Thank you Apostle Ifeoma and Reverend Daniel Fiiriter. Thank You, Jesus, for Robe of Righteousness Ministries Int'l. It's making a real difference in my life and family"— G.E., Liverpool.

"*B*efore I came to the **R.O.R.M.I. Southport Healing Glory Rally on Saturday, 28th October 2017,** I was feeling quite down and troubled. I was feeling quite anxious because things were not quite right around me.

So, I lifted myself up to the Lord, and He came through. And bit by bit, it went. They were like waves that went through me very slowly, very joyfully, and things began to iron themselves out. I was getting overworked by trying to do so many things at the same time.

And God, through His lovely word that came through the manifestation of His power, as Apostle Ifeoma reached out and put her hand on me. Through that joyful encounter, the Lord came down, and I felt Him go through me.

And out came out all the cry. The cry of joy! The cry that I was free! The cry that I was feeling so much better! And yes, I rejoiced. I came out of that meeting with so many blessings and so much joy.

And from that day forward, I have had so many blessings and so much joy. I have prayed over others every day because we have authority. And they are starting to see the same light with the Lord coming through for them, and they are being healed. It is going around, and it is so joyful.

I have never felt so much joy than I have felt with the Lord through Apostle Ifeoma, and these lovely meetings. And I am looking forward so much to what the Lord is going to do today.

Thank you very much. Absolutely beautiful! I love the Lord and I can't get enough of Him. It's really A heart-rendering feeling with the Lord. It's a love that no person, nobody or nothing can defeat the feeling I have for my Jesus and my God. I love Him"—D.H., Southport.

"*I* am so full of joy and overwhelmed by the goodness of God. Thank you, Apostle Ifeoma, for the prayers at the **R.O.R.M.I. Southport Healing Glory Outpouring Rally** on Saturday 25th November 2017. The Lord gave me victory through your prayers.

I had been facing attacks on my mind, which was really affecting me. When you prayed for me, I felt so much joy and freedom in my spirit. I could not stop laughing. I just could not stop. The presence of God was so heavy and strong.

Such a heavy wind of His presence in our midst! Other people began to laugh as well. Thank You Jesus. It was laughter of healing, deliverance and victory. I am so grateful to have come to this meeting. Glory be to God"—G.C., Liverpool.

THE FAVOUR DIMENSION

"*I* have been coming to the Eminent Ladies Club meetings for two years. And each time I came, it's been a great blessing.

When I came to the ELC August 2010 Worship & Healing Meeting, I was really burdened and troubled. I had incessant negative thoughts raging in my mind. Ironically, you look calm and well-dressed, but in fact, you actually feel like a wreck inside.

After the Praise & Worship, Rev. Ifeoma prayed for me as I responded to a word of knowledge she gave about someone suffering from depression. As she prayed, I fell under the power of God and had a tremendous encounter with the Lord.

I got up feeling completely different, completely peaceful—not a superficial one. My whole body and mind became entirely peaceful. The thoughts which were like 'jumping about' and hounding my mind were all gone. I also knew the depression which I had earlier, and which is really an illness, and which tried to put its grip on me was also gone.

So, I advise anyone going through a similar problem like I did, to come to these Meetings to get prayed for, and or ring Rev. Ifeoma for prayer, and God will heal you.

Prior to this Meeting, I woke up in my flat that morning feeling terribly bad, but with that encounter I had with the Lord, I feel entirely different—totally healed and peaceful"—J.M., Manchester.

"*In* 2016, I enrolled on a Master's degree Programme

for Social Work. I was expecting to get a full bursary to pay for the course but it did not happen. I was thinking of giving up.

But I thank God for Apostle Ifeoma, who prayed for me, and encouraged me to not give up, but rather look up to God, and expect His favour and mercy to sustain me.

Praise God! I got a grant from the University. This grant was very useful to cover some of my rent. This was money that came when I really needed it. And I thank God for that with all my heart. God has been taking care of me just like Apostle Ifeoma said.

I thank you, Apostle Ifeoma, servant of the Most High God, for your prayers. God has destroyed my frustrations and favoured me because of your prayers, wisdom, and encouragement to trust in God's unfailing kindness. Praise the Lord Jesus!

As I write this testimony, I am so full of joy and thanksgiving to God. When I later contacted the City Council, they told me that they sent a payment to my landlord for my rent. God is providing, Amen. They also said that they will be paying my rent every week directly to my landlord.

Not only that, but I was also told that they owed me some money and will make arrangements to pay me. I give glory to God because this is an awesome testimony for me. I can have more time to focus on my studies and don't have to feel pressured to be out working all the time.

Now in my second year of my course, God has

answered your timely prayers again for me to get extra funding to help me throughout the academic year. The University has awarded me a huge grant. This is such good news for me and will go a long way in supporting me in completing my studies.

My daughter has also received a yearly bus pass to use for school and all her school meals are paid for. I appreciate your prayers. Thank you, mighty Woman of God!

May I also seize this opportunity to praise and thank God for enabling me and my daughter to attend the Eminent Ladies International Conference 2017, themed, **"The Favour Dimension."** I came to the conference expecting the outpouring of God's favour in my life. I was so blessed at the conference. The messages spoken by the speakers were awesome. The presence of God was awesome amongst us.

On Sunday, the day after the conference, I decided to write a letter of complaint to my bank asking them to restore all the money they had taken from my account in the form of bank charges.

I sent this letter believing and thanking God for favour. Two days after, on Tuesday, the bank manager rang me on my mobile phone to say that they had seen my complaint and they decided to refund all the money they had taken for this year. He also cancelled the charge which was due to leave my account that day. Glory be to God!

To top it up, the same day, the University sent me an email stating that they had sent to my account a substantial sum of money. Praise Jesus! I had applied for the summer grant, and they stated I was late in making an application and the funding of this grant is very limited.

However, they decided to overlook this and send me the money anyway! I thank the Lord for the favour released upon me and my household at the Conference. I am so thankful for this incredible blessing and I know more and more are coming my way.

Since coming to the Eminent Ladies Int'l Conference in Manchester, God has poured out so much favour on me. In addition to all other blessings God granted me, I got some surprise money from the Inland Revenue.

This was indeed a pleasant surprise and I give glory to God! I also received my first order in my business franchise which is really incredible and I am thanking the Lord Jesus for more orders and customers.

In addition, I have been in need of a new cooker, washing machine and fridge. My washing machine had broken down, causing me to wash my clothes and my daughter's by hand. The cooker and the fridge were not in good condition. I decided to apply for the items at a voluntary organisation, but they rejected the application.

The Lord led me to apply to the Council for the items. The lady told me over the phone that they do not usually replace broken items as a rule, however she will help me to apply anyway, and I will have to see if they will approve it or not.

I thank God, I got a call the following Friday from

the Council, stating that they approved my application. They would be sending me a brand new cooker, washing machine and fridge, and they would also pay for the installation of all the items, and I did not have to pay a single penny towards it! As stated, they came, delivered and installed the items for me.

I thank God for this stream of favour that I have been swimming in. I know for sure it is because of the grace of God upon R.O.R.M.I. I appreciate R.O.R.M.I., and I am so glad to be part of this global Ministry.

I encourage people to partner with this anointed Ministry. R.O.R.M.I. is fertile ground, and partnering with this Ministry will bring so many blessings into their lives and others.

I also encourage people to come to the Meetings when they are advertised, sow or invest in the execution of the meetings and projects, as the Lord leads them. I thank God for the hosting of the Favour Dimension Conference, and enabling me to attend it. Glory be to God!"---E.G.

I praise God for all of these glorious reports shared in this chapter. Know that God is not a Respecter of persons.

So begin to declare now that His favour is coming upon you like never before. Once again, I release that anointing of favour to come upon you mightily now in Jesus name. Receive it, and begin to thank God for its manifestation in all of the places you want it to impact.

Assuming that you are a child of God, here is a daily prophetic prayer to access God's favour:

PRAYER:

"Father, I thank You that I am alive today. I thank You for Your glorious plans for my life—plans to prosper me in every way and not to harm me. I declare that I am highly favoured of You, and all I set my hands to do greatly prosper in Jesus name.

Father, Your favour is coming upon my life now, manifesting in peace and joy of answered prayer, You fighting my battles for me and giving me total victory over all my enemies.

Through Your favour, I receive supernatural recognition and acceptance, promotion, prosperity, productivity, increased assets in my life, debts cancelled (if applicable), wealth transfer to me, perfect health, open doors, total restoration, protection, long-life, pay-rise, increased business sales, good success, and blessings on my life.

I plead the blood of Jesus Christ upon my life and declare that I and all that pertains to me are covered with the blood of Jesus Christ, my link to Your shield of favour. Daily, I am increasing in wisdom and stature and in favour with God and men (Luke 2:52).

Today, I expect to be greatly favoured by You, and by men and women who will bless my life exceedingly. I expect Your favour to overwhelm me, transforming my life for good and filling my heart with uncommon joy. I receive it and thank You for it in Jesus name.

THE FAVOUR DIMENSION

Amen!"

If you are not yet saved or born again, now is the time to do so. Remember, favour is from God. He is the God of covenant who has paid the price through the precious blood of Jesus Christ, shed on the cross of Calvary for you to be saved.

All you need to do now is to receive God's primary gift of favour to you, the salvation of your soul, by simply and sincerely **praying this prayer aloud with your mouth:**

"Heavenly Father, I come to You in the name of Jesus Christ. I ask You to forgive my sins. I believe that Jesus died on the cross for my sins. I also believe that He was buried, and was raised from the dead on the third day so that I can be reconciled to You, being right in Your sight. Cleanse me with the blood of Jesus.

Lord Jesus, come into my heart and make me Your child. Fill me with Your Holy Spirit. Fill me with Your peace, and Your love, and Your power, and help me to live a life that will please You. Thank You Father for saving me and making me Your child in Jesus name! Amen"

Congratulations, if you have just confessed the prayer above! You can write to us by post or email me at **robeofrighteousness@btinternet.com** and request our free brochure, "Follow on to Know the Lord— Practical Guidelines for New Believers."

I encourage you to also get my anointed and insightful book, **Treasures Of The Brand New Man.** This book contains vital nuggets to help you begin and maximize your new life in Christ. Visit, **www. favourbooksandmusic.com** to obtain this book. But, if you cannot afford it, write us to let us know, and we will send it to you free of charge,

Email: robeofrighteousness@btinternet.com.

Dear reader, before I round up this chapter, to help you further see yourself in your new identity as a favoured child of God, I want to give you the words of my song, **"Favour Is My Name"**, the title track of my **Songs Of Glory 6 Music CD Album:** "Favour is my name. Favour is my name. Favour is my name. Favour is my name. Favour from the Lord."

This song carries an awesome anointing of favour on it. I already shared the story of how I received it in **chapter 5** of this book. I believe this song will have a profound impact on you as you daily meditate on its words.

Better still, I encourage you get this anointed CD Album, containing this song and other 15 amazing, authentic songs of glory downloaded to me directly by the Holy Spirit, ministering to mans' needs.

It will be a great addition to your worship library collection. This Album can be ordered from our website, **http:www.favourbooksandmusic.com.** Enjoy this amazing testimony about this album:

"Wow amazing treadmill workout this morning to some Spirit lifting music, **Songs of Glory 6 CD Worship Album, FAVOUR IS MY NAME,** by my Beloved Sister Ifeoma. Loved running to the song, **Worthy Worthy.**

THE FAVOUR DIMENSION

Imagined I was running my race for Him, telling Father, "I'm moving all obstacles out my path! Keeping the Cross before me, my ultimate reminder of the acne of His saving Grace. Eventually cooling down to a walk to the song, **You Are Worthy My God."**

At one point, I had to stop and just worship because I was lifted into the Throne room of Grace. Oh, what Glory shone! What peace surrounded me! And at that point, He filled me afresh with His Holy Spirit.

So I said to my Father Abba, "I'll be back later on tonight for a double portion of the very same. All Power and Glory Be to His Name" And thank you, Beloved Ifeoma, for this powerful Gift. May our Father God richly bless you with all spiritual Blessings"—P.T. Leicester.

CHAPTER 8

A FINAL WORD

I believe that we have covered a lot on favour and its awesome benefits in one's life in this book. We have touched on some benefits of God's exceeding abundant grace. We have also looked at real life testimonials of favour.

Although we don't work to earn God's favour, I still want to observe that we need to position ourselves daily to receive from the streams of God's favour being poured out each day towards our direction.

We need to guard every favour manifested to us by walking in holiness, and in God's wisdom, love, and humility. Know that pride and sin can instantly terminate the flow of favour into our lives.

As a safeguard, I encourage you to set yourself apart to deepen your walk with God, in wisdom and integrity. Intensify your worship of Him. Make Him, His presence, and His word your greatest priority pursuit.

These divine acts will help to trigger and sustain the flow of favour in and through your life. Remember, God loves to surround those who love Him with His favour (Psalm 5:12).

So devote each day to seek His face through the help of the Holy Spirit, in prayer, worship, and studying of

THE FAVOUR DIMENSION

His word. Incorporate times of fasting in your walk with God, as this sharpens your spiritual man and makes you more sensitive to discern God's voice and the flow of His favour into your life, so you can maximize those moments.

Let "your speech always *be* with grace, seasoned with salt, that you may know how you ought to answer each one" (Colossians 4:5-6). Having prepared yourself, go ahead to intentionally declare God's favour upon your life regularly in every way.

Speak His covenant blessings upon your life each new day and expect them to manifest and dominate your life to His glory. Expect to be favoured by God. Trust Him in all your undertakings to unleash His favour upon you and all that pertains to you.

Be persuaded that the Lord truly encompasses the righteous with favour as with a shield, and by His favour He will strengthen you in all areas of your life (Psalm 5:12; 30:7).

As I conclude this book, **I want to now pray a prayer of impartation of favour upon you:**

"Father, I release Your impartation of favour upon your son/daughter who is reading this book in Jesus name. I decree that they are increased in wisdom and stature and in favour with God and men (Luke 2:52).

Father, let Your favour go before them and level the mountains before them, break down the gates of bronze, and cut through the bars of iron blocking their inheritance in Jesus name.

I release them to arise and take ownership of the

treasures of darkness, riches stored up in secret places, so that they may know and testify to all that You are the Lord.

Daily, their eyes and trust will be fixed upon You, and Your favour will surround them as they allow You to lead them in the way to go, so they can excel and profit in life and be able to serve as Your effective workmanship, advancing Your kingdom on earth to Your glory (Isaiah 45:2-3; Psalm 5:12; Isaiah 48:17; Ephesians 2:10, in context).

Daily, Your favour will serve as a major shield to them, a weapon of victory, protection, provision, beautification and blessing to them. I decree that all their needs are met through Your favour supply in Jesus name." RECEIVE IT IN JESUS NAME! Amen.

Remember, as I mentioned earlier on in this book, favour is positively contagious. So, as you receive it, allow it to get to others through you. **Remember David and Dorcas?**

Both received favour in their days and respectively planted it purposefully into the houses of God of their day. Consequently, they received great harvests of favour in return.

David "found favor before God and asked to find a dwelling for the God of Jacob ... From this man's seed, according to *the* promise, God raised up for Israel a Savior—Jesus" (Acts 7:46; 13:23)).

Not only did God preserve David from danger through His favour, but He also enabled David to distinguish himself as a great leader whose legacy still lives on. Besides, He gave him the privilege to be an ancestor of our Lord, Jesus Christ.

Dorcas was full of good works and charitable deeds which she did in the house of God (Acts 9:36). Dorcas, on the other hand, as I mentioned earlier, was supernaturally raised from the dead at a time she least expected it.

May I also add that Cornelius, the Roman centurion's prayers and generous almsgiving were remembered by God. Consequently, he received God's favoured priceless salvation for him and his household, a gift that ultimately reached and impacted the Gentile race (See Acts 10:1-6, 30-32, 44-48).

Whatever a man sows he shall also reap (Galatians 6:7). When you sow favour, you reap a greater harvest of favour in return. And "let us not grow weary while doing good, for in due season we shall reap if we do not lose heart. Therefore, as we have opportunity, let us do good to all, especially to those who are of the household of faith" (Galatians 6:9-10).

So, if God has blessed you in any way through this book, write and share your testimony with me. Also, may I encourage you to partner with our Ministry, **Robe Of Righteousness Ministries Int'l,** so as to join us to spread the unlimited fragrance of God's love and healing glory to the ends of the earth sustainably.

Visit our website, **http://www.rormi.org.uk** now and plant your precious seed into this fertile, favour-soaked soil of Almighty God. Keep in mind that one thrust of harvest of favour in your direction can transform your life and all that pertains to you for good.

You can also let this outpouring of favour unleashed upon you through this book keep getting wider and wider and impact more lives globally to the glory of God by investing to get a copy for someone dear to you, and encourage others to get it too.

Join me and let's get this anointed word out through this book to many globally to God's glory. Once again, do let me hear of the glorious breakthroughs the Lord manifests to you in the coming days through the revelations and impartations you have received from this book, so I can rejoice with you.

Until then, Keep Walking In The Favour Dimension—It's The Best Path To Thread On!

THE FAVOUR DIMENSION

Order now on

www.FavourBooksAndMusic.com

or FavourLandBooks on Amazon or from Waterstones, Blackwells or your local bookstore. Books also available in Kindle on Amazon.

Connect on Facebook:

www.Facebook.com/FavourBooksAndMusic

PRAYER REQUEST

Send your prayer request by email to info@rormi.org.uk, or call our Glory Prayer Line on (U.K.) +44 (0)161 2736597.

PARTNERSHIP

You can make financial donations to support the vision and projects of the Robe of Righteousness Ministries International by visiting **http://www.rormi.org.uk** OR contact the Ministry on +44 (0)161 2736597.

OR Email:- info@rormi.org.uk

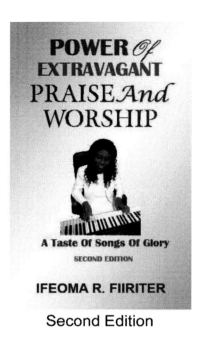

POWER *Of*
EXTRAVAGANT
PRAISE *And*
WORSHIP

A Taste Of Songs Of Glory

SECOND EDITION

IFEOMA R. FIIRITER

Second Edition

Order now on
www.FavourBooksAndMusic.com
or FavourLandBooks on Amazon or from Waterstones,
Blackwells or your local bookstore. Books also available in
Kindle on Amazon.

Connect on Facebook:
www.Facebook.com/FavourBooksAndMusic

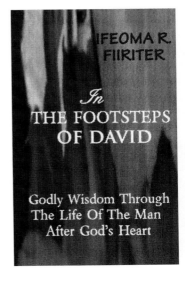

Order now on

www.FavourBooksAndMusic.com

Connect on Facebook:
www.Facebook.com/FavourBooksAndMusic.

Wind Of The Holy Ghost CD Album is also available on iTunes, Amazon, Spotify, Google Play, & other Networks.

GOD OF	WIND OF THE
BREAKTHROUGH	HOLY GHOST

Songs Of Glory Music CDs

Order now on

www.FavourBooksAndMusic.com

Connect on Facebook:

www.Facebook.com/FavourBooksAndMusic

SONGS OF GLORY - FAVOUR IS MY NAME DVD

Songs Of Glory Music CDs

**GREAT IS THE
LORD OUR GOD**

**HALLELUJAH!
OUR GOD REIGNS**

Order now on

www.FavourBooksAndMusic.com

Connect on Facebook:
www.Facebook.com/FavourBooksAndMusic

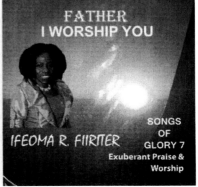

Songs Of Glory Music CDs / Book

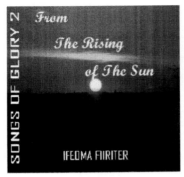

**BE ENTHRONED
O LORD**

**FROM THE RISING
OF THE SUN**

Order now on
www.FavourBooksAndMusic.com
Book can also be obtained from FavourLandBooks on
Amazon,
Connect on Facebook:
www.Facebook.com/FavourBooksAndMusic

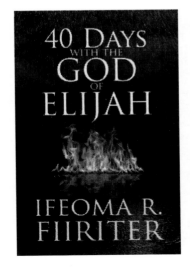

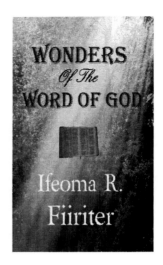

Order now on

www.FavourBooksAndMusic.com

or FavourLandBooks on Amazon or from Waterstones,
Blackwells or your local bookstore. Books also available in
Kindle on Amazon.

Connect on Facebook:

www.Facebook.com/FavourBooksAndMusic

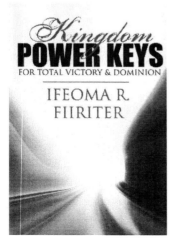

Your Prophetic Breakthrough Prayer Capsules For Dominion
Paperback and Audiobook

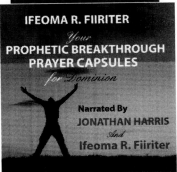

Order now on

www.FavourBooksAndMusic.com
or FavourLandBooks on Amazon or from Waterstones,
Blackwells or your local bookstore.
Connect on Facebook:
www.Facebook.com/FavourBooksAndMusic
Order Digital Format from Audible using
this link: http://bit.ly/PrayerCapsules

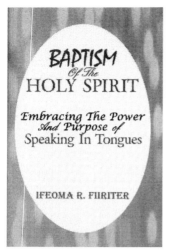

Order now on

www.FavourBooksAndMusic.com

or FavourLandBooks on Amazon or from Waterstones, Blackwells or your local bookstore.

Connect on Facebook:

www.Facebook.com/FavourBooksAndMusic

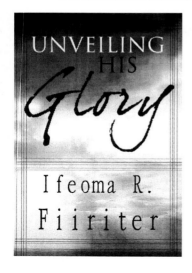

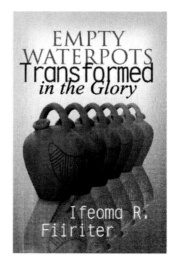

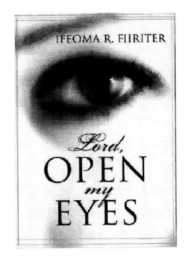

Order now on

www.FavourBooksAndMusic.com
or FavourLandBooks on Amazon or from Waterstones,
Blackwells or your local bookstore.

KEYS TO SUCCESSFUL WAITING ON THE LORD

FROM LODEBAR TO THE PALACE

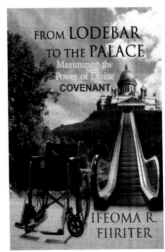

Order now on

www.FavourBooksAndMusic.com
or FavourLandBooks on Amazon or from Waterstones,
Blackwells or your local bookstore.

Connect on Facebook:
www.Facebook.com/FavourBooksAndMusic

**TREASURES OF THE
BRAND NEW MAN**

**GOD'S WEAPONS
OF WARFARE**

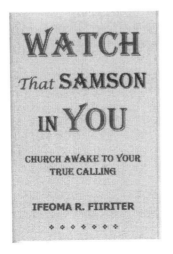

Order now on
**www.
FavourBooksAndMusic.
com**
or FavourLandBooks
on Amazon or from
Waterstones, Blackwells or
your local bookstore.

Connect on Facebook:
**www.Facebook.com/
FavourBooksAndMusic**

ABOUT THE AUTHOR

Rev. (Mrs) Ifeoma R. Fiiriter is an end-time Apostle and Visionary, a Woman of Prayer, and a Psalmist with a strong prophetic edge to her ministry. Her passion for God, His presence and His word, has given her intense insight into the heavenly realm. She has also been uniquely endowed by God with great grace, wisdom, and other gifts of the Holy Spirit which empower her to effectively serve Him in many capacities in the Body of Christ and in the marketplace.

She is Co-founder & Overseer of the Robe of Righteousness Ministries International, a ministry on the cutting edge of God's global glory outpouring, spreading the unlimited fragrance of His love, glory, healing, and revival to the nations. She is the Founder & President of the Eminent Ladies Club, an international, inter-denominational ministry committed to raising women to active, victorious, Christian faith and witness.

Alongside her husband, Rev. Daniel, she shepherds the Tabernacle of Glory Church and hosts dynamic R.O.R.M.I. Healing Glory Outpouring Rallies. She also hosts anointed and lively Facebook Live broadcasts, impacting many lives globally. Apostle Ifeoma Fiiriter is an Entrepreneur, a Publisher, Wisdom Coach, Conference Speaker, and a prolific Writer.

She is the Author of twenty nine life-changing books, including, "God's Extravagant Goodness, Potent Secrets Of Breakthrough Prayer; In The Footsteps Of David, Honey From the Wilderness; Wisdom Is The Principal Thing:

Maximizing The Treasure Of Divine Wisdom; Unveiling His Glory; Lord, Open My Eyes; 40 Days With the God of Elijah; and Your Prophetic Breakthrough Capsules For Dominion."

Apostle Ifeoma Fiiriter is an Anointed Musician and Psalmist of God. She has written over **1,630 Songs of Glory** downloaded to her by the Holy Spirit in over twenty years of intensely seeking the Lord in communion and worship. She has produced one musical video and published a Songbook and devotional guide, **Songs Of Glory Vol. One: 1,012 Heavenly Downloads Of The Holy Spirit From The Throne Of Grace.**

She has recorded **15** authentic **Songs Of Glory CD Albums**, including, "Lord God Almighty; The Bride Of Christ; You Wiped Away My Tears; One Moment In The Glory; God Of Breakthrough; Sound Of The Latter Rain; Wind Of The Holy Ghost; Favour Is My Name; Only YOU Can Satisfy; Great Is The LORD Our GOD; and Let Your Fire Fall, LORD."

Her strong, anointed prayer, worship lifestyle, and ministry, coupled with her bold, compassionate and powerful proclamation of the gospel, is accompanied with signs, wonders and miracles. Her anointed ministry resources are freeing innumerable lives world-wide from satanic yokes, establishing them in the kingdom of God, and helping them to fulfil their destinies.

Apostle Ifeoma's simple, practical, and dynamic ministry style endears her to the hearts of a broad spectrum of people. She holds an M.A. Degree in English Language; PG. Dip. Film & TV Production; and a Ministerial Diploma